ROSA PARKS

ROSA PARKS

A Biography

Joyce A. Hanson

GREENWOOD BIOGRAPHIES

GREENWOOD

AN IMPRINT OF ABC-CLIO, LLC
Santa Barbara, California • Denver, Colorado • Oxford, England

Copyright 2011 by Joyce A. Hanson

Library of Congress Cataloging-in-Publication Data

Hanson, Joyce Ann.
  Rosa Parks : a biography / Joyce A. Hanson.
    p. cm. — (Greenwood biographies)
  Includes bibliographical references and index.
    ISBN 978-0-313-35217-1 (hardcopy : alk. paper) — ISBN 978-0-313-
35218-8 (ebook)   1. Parks, Rosa, 1913–2005.   2. African American women
civil rights workers—Alabama—Montgomery—Biography.   3. Civil rights
workers—Alabama—Montgomery—Biography.   4. African Americans—Civil
rights—Alabama—Montgomery—History—20th century.   5. Segregation in
transportation—Alabama—Montgomery—History—20th century.   6. Montgomery
(Ala.)—Race relations.   7. Montgomery (Ala.)—Biography.   I. Title.
  F334.M753P3737 2011
  323.092—dc22
  [B]   2011010867

ISBN: 978-0-313-35217-1
EISBN: 978-0-313-35218-8

15   14   13   12   11   1   2   3   4   5

This book is also available on the World Wide Web as an eBook.
Visit www.abc-clio.com for details.

Greenwood
An Imprint of ABC-CLIO, LLC

ABC-CLIO, LLC
130 Cremona Drive, P.O. Box 1911
Santa Barbara, California 93116-1911

This book is printed on acid-free paper ∞

Manufactured in the United States of America

CONTENTS

CONTENTS

SERIES FOREWORD

In response to high school and public library needs, Greenwood developed this distinguished series of full-length biographies specifically for student use. Prepared by field experts and professionals, these engaging biographies are tailored for high school students who need challenging yet accessible biographies. Ideal for secondary school assignments, the length, format and subject areas are designed to meet educators' requirements and students' interests.

Greenwood offers an extensive selection of biographies spanning all curriculum-related subject areas including social studies, the sciences, literature and the arts, history and politics, as well as popular culture, covering public figures and famous personalities from all time periods and backgrounds, both historic and contemporary, who have made an impact on American and/or world culture. Greenwood biographies were chosen based on comprehensive feedback from librarians and educators. Consideration was given to both curriculum relevance and inherent interest. The result is an intriguing mix of the well known and the unexpected, the saints and sinners from long-ago history and contemporary pop culture. Readers will find a wide array of subject choices from fascinating crime figures like Al Capone to inspiring pioneers like Margaret Mead, from the greatest minds of our time like Stephen Hawking to the most amazing success stories of our day like J. K. Rowling.

While the emphasis is on fact, not glorification, the books are meant to be fun to read. Each volume provides in-depth information about the subject's life from birth through childhood, the teen years, and adulthood. A thorough account relates family background and education, traces personal and professional influences, and explores struggles, accomplishments, and contributions. A time line highlights the most significant life events against a historical perspective. Bibliographies supplement the reference value of each volume.

ACKNOWLEDGMENTS

Every historian who takes on the work of writing a book accumulates a sizable scholarly debt, for although writing is a solitary process, completing research and producing a book is a group effort. This work is no exception. I would like to thank all of the archivists at the many sites I used in my research for their dedication to scholarly research as well as their valuable help in locating and suggesting sources. California State University, San Bernardino, and the History Department gave a most important resource: funding. Thanks to Mini-Grant and internal department funding, I was able to travel to use the E. D. Nixon Collection and the Montgomery Improvement Association Papers, Special Collections at the Levi Watkins Library, Alabama State University, Montgomery; the Eugene W. Carter Papers at the Alabama State Archives; and, most importantly, the Rosa L. Parks Papers at the Walter Reuther Archives of Labor and Urban Affairs, at Wayne State University in Detroit.

Thanks as well to my two colleagues and best friends: Cheryl Riggs and Kent Schofield, who continue to support and encourage my research projects, but more importantly give freely of their time, listen to my laments, and offer thoughtful comments and observations.

This project would not have been possible without Sandy Towers, who suggested the idea and nurtured me through the two years it took to complete the work.

Finally, no project can be brought to a successful conclusion without the support of my wonderful family: Jen, Mike, Ali, Erik, Maggie, and, most of all, my wonderful husband, Jim. His job is to keep me laughing—a job for which he is eminently qualified and that he always accomplishes.

INTRODUCTION

On December 1, 1955, when Rosa Parks refused to give up her seat to a white man on the segregated Cleveland Avenue bus, she touched off a 381-day boycott of the city's bus system. Almost immediately, Parks became a civil rights icon, and many misconceptions about her background and motivations were born. These were, in part, perpetuated by Parks herself. In an article in *Ebony* magazine, Parks recalled, "I really don't know why I wouldn't move. There was no plan at all. I was just tired from shopping. My feet hurt."[1] While Parks certainly did not plan to challenge the segregation laws on that day, she was not a tired little old lady turned accidental hero. Mrs. Parks was only 42 years old and no more tired than usual after a long day at work. More importantly, she was an experienced local civil rights activist and had been the secretary of the local Montgomery branch of the National Association for the Advancement of Colored People (NAACP) since 1943. She had worked in other civil rights actions, in voter registration campaigns, and as an adviser to the NAACP Youth Council.[2] Rosa Parks did not simply wander into history. Her actions followed a rational course and placed her within a significant group of African American women activists who struggled against white supremacy and for racial and social justice in the United States.

These women have long been ignored by the media and historians, remaining virtually unknown to most Americans. However, African American women have a long history of organizing associations to improve conditions in their communities, initiating civil rights campaigns, and challenging discrimination. They were antilynching crusaders, teachers, and labor union activists; they worked in politics and journalism, led religious groups, and were plaintiffs and lawyers in many civil rights court cases. Beginning in the 19th century, the actions in which they engaged laid the foundation for the modern civil rights movement. In the 1950s and 1960s, they became the backbone of that modern movement. Nevertheless, because they were not the official leaders of organizations such as the Southern Christian Leadership Conference (SCLC), the NAACP, or the Congress of Racial Equality (CORE), their contributions remained obscure. The image of the civil rights movement does not match historical reality.[3]

The reasons for African American women's involvement in the struggle for equality and social justice were both personal and political. Their activities were often based on an emotional response to inequality, leading to spontaneous actions and using existing networks to lay the foundations for a movement. Many of these actions centered on the treatment to which black women were subject on public transportation. As early as the end of the Civil War, African American women began to challenge unequal treatment on public conveyances. For example, in March 1865, while abolitionist Sojourner Truth was in Washington, D.C.—counseling, teaching, and helping to resettle freed slaves—the city enacted a law that forbade streetcar conductors to exclude passengers based upon race. Few African Americans were daring enough to test this new law, but Sojourner Truth did indeed do so. One day, Truth entered a streetcar and the conductor attempted to remove her, slamming her against the door in the process. Truth then had the conductor arrested for violating the antisegregation law, brought the case to trial, and won.[4] Sojourner Truth became the first black woman to test the legality of segregation in Washington, D.C.

Southern states were not the only places where black women faced segregation on public transportation. In 1868, Mary Ellen Pleasant, an abolitionist and businesswoman in San Francisco, California, challenged segregationist practices with her lawsuit against the North Beach

Railroad Company. When a driver refused to allow Pleasant to board a streetcar because she was black, Pleasant sued, and the court awarded her $500 in damages. Unfortunately, the appeals court overturned the award,[5] but Pleasant was successful in bringing discrimination to the attention of the community.

Perhaps the best-known African American woman activist of the late 19th century was Ida B. Wells. A teacher, journalist, co-owner of the Memphis *Free Speech and Headlight,* and antilynching crusader, Wells encouraged blacks to leave the South rather than submit to segregation—or, if they were unwilling to leave, to fight back mainly through economic pressure. At her urging, thousands of African Americans boycotted Memphis's newly opened and segregated streetcar line. In addition to encouraging others to boycott, Wells fought segregation on public transportation individually as well. In 1883, when a conductor on the Memphis-to-Woodstock line of the Chesapeake, Ohio & Southwestern Railroad came to collect Wells's first-class ticket, he told her to move to the smoking car; this was the usual response to any black woman seated in first-class accommodations. At first Wells ignored the man, but after he collected all other tickets, he returned to Wells. He removed her bag and umbrella, saying that although he would treat her "like a lady," she would have to move to the other car. When Wells then refused to surrender her ticket or her seat, the conductor grabbed her by the arm and tried to remove her from her seat forcibly. She held onto the back of her seat, braced her feet on the seat in front of her, and bit his hand. Other passengers then came to the aid of the conductor and carried her out of the car. Rather than sit in the smoking car, Wells left the train at the next stop. The cheers of white passengers further humiliated her as she left the train. Wells, however, sued the railroad, and in May 1884 the Memphis Circuit Court awarded Wells $200 in damages. Again, in November 1884, a conductor refused to allow Wells to enter the first-class car and "put his hands upon her to push her back." Wells filed another lawsuit and again won. This time the court awarded her $500.[6] Despite these successes, Wells continued to have problems on the trains. As individuals, African American women had little power to overturn segregation.

Nannie Helen Burroughs, religious leader, educator, and civil rights activist, moved beyond individual protest. As head of the Women's

Auxiliary of the National Baptist Convention, Burroughs did not at first call for an end to "separate but equal"; she simply demanded "equal" facilities for African Americans. By 1918, Burroughs no longer endorsed simple equality in accommodations but rather argued for the desegregation of railroad transportation. "Nothing short of repeal of the separate laws is going to bring a permanent and satisfactory change in travel in those states where the law is in operation," Burroughs argued. The purpose of the segregated car, according to Burroughs, was to suggest the inferiority of one race and humiliate African Americans. In 1919, Burroughs used her formidable position within the National Baptist Convention to recommend that the black Baptist church dedicate the Sunday before Thanksgiving to fasting and prayer to protest the "undemocratic and un-Christian spirit of the United States as shown by its discriminating and barbarous treatment of colored people." Certainly, this single action would not overturn segregation in America, but it did give African Americans a way to speak out, as they would not do openly otherwise.[7] In 1934, Burroughs insisted that African Americans fight for their rights with "ballots and dollars." Burroughs's actions more widely publicized the issue of segregation and made it clear that African Americans were not willing to accept such treatment.

These are just a few of the stories illustrating African American women's actions against segregation in public transportation. Throughout the 20th century, black women continued to fight both individually and through their organizations against Jim Crow. In 1920, educator Charlotte Hawkins Brown sued the Pullman Railroad Car Company for racial discrimination, and rather than face a court battle, the Pullman Company offered Brown a $200 settlement.[8] In 1940, local law enforcement arrested civil rights activist Pauli Murray in Virginia for refusing to give up her seat on a Greyhound bus to a white person.[9] It is impossible to know if Mrs. Parks was aware of these events. However, we can be certain that she did know about prior activity in Montgomery, Alabama. As secretary of the NAACP, Rosa Parks kept meticulous records of the incidents involving discrimination and segregation, beginning in 1943. She knew that there was a history of arresting women for refusing to comply with segregation laws on the city bus system. In 1944, local police arrested and beat Viola White when she refused to sit in the back of a segregated bus. In 1949, Jo Ann Robinson, leader of the

Montgomery Women's Political Council, endured an abusive tirade by a white bus driver. In March 1955, local police arrested Claudette Colvin in Montgomery for refusing to give up her seat on a city bus.[10] Other cases involved Aurelia Shines Browder and 18-year-old Louise Smith. The local court fined both Browder and Smith for not obeying the bus drivers' requests that they give up their seats to white passengers.[11] Social change does not come about by the actions of one individual. It is the "product of deliberate, incremental action."[12] Rosa Parks stood on the shoulders of the women who came before her and was certainly aware of the actions taken by the women in Montgomery.

Other factors contributed to Parks's actions on that day as well. Family attitudes toward segregation, her teachers and educational experiences, her organizational memberships, the experiences of African Americans during World War II, rising violence against African Americans, presidential actions, and decisions of the U.S. Supreme Court would all play a part in Rosa Parks's decision to act. The following chapters explore these factors in depth. *What* Rosa Parks did was not unique; that it sparked a 381-day bus boycott and inspired later generations of activists is what sets Rosa Parks apart from those who came before her.

What made Rosa Parks different? Why did her refusal to give up her seat on the bus spark a mass movement? Her story has become legend, but because of that legend, the full story of her life as an activist remains unknown. Parks's actual story is much more interesting than the legend. As Paul Loeb has written,

> She began modestly, by attending one meeting and then another. Hesitant at first, she gained confidence as she spoke out. She kept on despite a profoundly uncertain context as she and others acted as best they could to challenge deeply entrenched injustices with little certainty of results. Had she and others given up after their 10th or 11th year of commitment, we might never have heard of the Montgomery boycott.[13]

People who have worked for social change are not saints, they were not born to greatness, they had doubts and fears. This is the story of Rosa Parks, a woman who, despite her fears and uncertainties, fought throughout her life to expand American democracy and create a more just society.

NOTES

1. Rosa L. Parks Papers, Walter Reuther Archives of Labor and Urban Affairs, Wayne State University, box 1, folder 1.

2. Rosa Parks, *My Story* (New York: Penguin Books, 1992), 81, 94.

3. Charles Payne, "Men Led, but Women Organized: Movement Participation of Women in the Mississippi Delta," in *Women in the Civil Rights Movement: Trailblazers and Torchbearers, 1941–1964*, ed. Vicki L. Crawford, Jacqueline Anne Rouse, and Barbara Woods (New York: Carlson Publishing, 1990), 1–12.

4. Olive Gilbert, *Narrative of Sojourner Truth: A Bondswoman of Olden Time, With a History of Her Labors and Correspondence Drawn from Her Book of Life* (New York: Penguin Books, 1998), 140–43, 183–99.

5. "Mary Ellen Pleasant," in *Black Women in America*, 2nd ed., vol. 2, ed. Darlene Clark Hine (New York: Oxford University Press, 2005), 507.

6. Linda O. McMurray, *To Keep the Waters Troubled: The Life of Ida B. Wells* (New York: Oxford University Press, 1998), 26–28.

7. Evelyn Brooks Higginbotham, *Righteous Discontent: The Women's Movement in the Black Baptist Church, 1880–1920* (Cambridge, MA: Harvard University Press, 1993), 223–24.

8. Charles W. Wadelington and Richard F. Knapp, *Charlotte Hawkins Brown and Palmer Memorial Institute: What One Young African American Woman Could Do* (Chapel Hill: University of North Carolina Press, 1999), 95–96.

9. Lynne Olson, *Freedom's Daughters: The Unsung Heroines of the Civil Rights Movement from 1830 to 1970* (New York: Simon and Schuster, 2001), 64.

10. "Civil Rights Movement," in *Black Women in America*, 2nd ed., vol. 2, ed. Darlene Clark Hine (New York: Oxford University Press, 2005), 236–37.

11. Randall K. Bush, "Remembering Rosa Parks: Recognizing a Contemporary Prophetic Act," *Theological Studies* 65 (2004): 841.

12. Paul Rogat Loeb, "Commentary; Ordinary People Produce Extraordinary Results; Heroism: Rather Than Mythologize Those Who Act for Justice, We Can Learn from What Empowered Them," *Los Angeles Times* January 14, 2000, 7.

13. Ibid.

TIMELINE: EVENTS IN THE LIFE OF ROSA PARKS

1896   The Supreme Court hands down its *Plessy v. Ferguson* decision, paving the way for the institution of repressive Jim Crow laws in the South.

1909   The National Association for the Advancement of Colored People (NAACP) is founded in New York by prominent black and white intellectuals.

1913   On February 4, Rosa McCauley is born in Tuskegee, Alabama. President Woodrow Wilson's administration initiates the racial segregation of workplaces, rest rooms, and lunchrooms in all federal offices across the nation.

1915   The Great Migration of African Americans from the South to northern cities begins.
       The Oklahoma Grandfather Clause is overturned in *Guinn v. United States*.
       William Simmons revives the Ku Klux Klan at Stone Mountain, Georgia.

1917   The United States enters World War I.
       Nearly 10,000 African Americans and their supporters march down Manhattan's Fifth Avenue on July 28 as part of a "silent

parade," an NAACP-organized protest against lynchings, race riots, and the denial of rights. This was the first major civil rights demonstration of the 20th century.

The U.S. Supreme Court in *Buchanan v. Warley* strikes down the Louisville, Kentucky, ordinance mandating segregated neighborhoods.

1918 The armistice between the Allies and Germany, signed on November 11, ends World War I Eighty-three African Americans are lynched during the year, including a number of returning soldiers still in uniform.

Rosa McCauley enters school in Pine Level, Alabama.

1919 Twenty-five race riots take place throughout the nation, prompting the term *Red Summer.*

1920 The Harlem Renaissance—a remarkable period of creativity for black writers, poets, and artists—begins.

1921 At least 60 blacks and 21 whites are killed in a race riot in Tulsa, Oklahoma.

1923 The small, predominately black town of Rosewood, Florida, is destroyed by a mob of white residents from nearby communities.

1924 Rosa McCauley begins attending school in Montgomery, Alabama, but is forced to leave in 1929 to care for her aging grandmother.

1931 The Scottsboro Boys are arrested in Alabama.

Raymond Parks becomes involved in the efforts to free them.

1932 On December 18, Rosa McCauley marries Raymond Parks in Pine Level, Alabama.

1933 Rosa Parks receives her high school diploma.

1935 In *Norris v. Alabama*, the U.S. Supreme Court rules that a defendant has the right to trial by a jury of his or her peers.

The Maryland Supreme Court rules in *Murray v. Pearson* that the University of Maryland must admit African Americans to its law school or establish a separate school for blacks. The University of Maryland chooses to admit its first black students.

1938 In *Missouri ex rel. Gaines v. Canada*, the U.S. Supreme Court rules that a state that provides in-state education for whites must provide comparable in-state education for blacks.

1941   On December 8, following the attack on Pearl Harbor on December 7, the United States enters World War II.

The U.S. Army creates the Tuskegee Air Squadron, made up entirely of black airmen.

1943   Rosa Parks becomes secretary of the Montgomery NAACP.

Rosa Parks tries to register to vote and is denied.

The Detroit race riot claims 34 lives, including 25 African Americans. Other riots occur in Harlem, New York City; Mobile, Alabama; and Beaumont, Texas.

1944   Rosa Parks again tries to register to vote and is again denied.

Rosa Parks refuses to give up her seat and is ejected from a racially segregated bus.

1945   Rosa Parks tries to register to vote for a third time and receives her voter registration card.

World War II ends.

1946   Rosa Parks attends an NAACP leadership conference run by Ella Baker.

The U.S. Supreme Court in *Morgan v. Virginia* rules that segregation in interstate bus travel is unconstitutional.

President Harry S. Truman sends the FBI to investigate the lynching at Moore's Ford.

President Truman establishes a civil rights commission; their report, titled *To Secure These Rights*, is issued.

Sylvester McCauley, Rosa Parks's brother, moves to Detroit.

1948   President Truman issues Executive Order 9981 directing the desegregation of the armed forces.

1949   Rosa Parks becomes adviser to the NAACP's Youth Council.

1951   The U.S. Supreme Court rules that racial segregation in restaurants in the District of Columbia is unconstitutional.

1953   African Americans in Baton Rouge, Louisiana, begin a boycott of their city's segregated municipal bus line.

1954   The U.S. Supreme Court in *Brown v. Board of Education* declares that segregation in all U.S. public schools is unconstitutional, nullifying the earlier judicial doctrine of separate but equal.

1955   Rosa Parks attends a workshop at Highlander Folk School on implementing the *Brown* decision; there she meets Myles Horton and Septima Clark.

Emmett Till is brutally murdered in Mississippi in August. Two white men charged with the crime are acquitted by an all-white jury.

In August, Rosa Parks meets Martin Luther, King, Jr., for the first time.

Rosa Parks refuses to relinquish her bus seat to a white man on December 1, initiating the Montgomery Bus Boycott. Martin Luther King, Jr., becomes leader of the boycott. The nonviolent, direct-action phase of the civil rights movement begins.

The homes of Martin Luther King, Jr., and E. D. Nixon homes are bombed.

1956   Rosa Parks loses her job at the Montgomery Fair department store.

Autherine Lucy is admitted to the University of Alabama; after riots erupt, she is expelled.

In *Gayle v. Browder*, the U.S. Supreme Court bans segregation in intrastate travel, giving a victory to those supporting the Montgomery Bus Boycott.

1957   Governor Orval Faubus blocks the admission of nine black students at Central High School in Little Rock, Arkansas; federal troops and the National Guard are called to intervene on behalf of the students, who become known as the Little Rock Nine.

Rosa Parks moves to Detroit. Thereafter, she takes a job as hostess at the Holly Tree Inn at Hampton Institute in Virginia.

1958   At a book signing in Harlem, Martin Luther King, Jr., is stabbed by Izola Ware Curry.

1959   Rosa Parks leaves Hampton Institute and returns to Detroit; she takes a job at the Stockton Sewing Company and meets Elaine Eason Steele.

Dr. Martin Luther King, Jr., established the Southern Christian Leadership Conference (SCLC) in Atlanta and becomes its first president.

1960   On February 1, four black students from North Carolina Agricultural and Technical College begin the sit-in movement at a Woolworth's lunch counter in Greensboro. Their action leads to a massive grassroots sit-in movement by students throughout the South.

Ella Baker organizes a meeting of activist students at Shaw University in Raleigh, North Carolina, where students establish the Student Non-Violent Coordinating Committee (SNCC).

1961   The Congress of Racial Equality (CORE) begins Freedom Rides in an effort to desegregate interstate travel.

1962   Mississippi governor Ross Barnett blocks the admission of James
Meredith to the University of Mississippi in Oxford. President John F. Kennedy sends 320 U.S. marshals to ensure Meredith's safety on campus. Rioting on campus kills 2 and injures 375. Finally, 30,000 federal troops are sent to Oxford to end the violence and rioting.

1963   The SCLC begins demonstrations in Birmingham, Alabama. Sheriff Eugene "Bull" Connor responds with violence. Attack dogs, tear gas, cattle prods, and fire hoses are used against the demonstrators. Public parks and playgrounds are closed to avoid integration.
Whites bomb the homes of various African Americans involved in the campaign.
The 16th Street Baptist Church is bombed in Birmingham, Alabama, killing four girls ages 11 to 14: Addie Mae Collins, Denise McNair, Carole Robertson, and Cynthia Wesley.
In Jackson, Mississippi, NAACP Field Secretary Medgar Evers is killed in an ambush outside his home.
On August 28, more than 200,000 civil rights advocates hold a March on Washington to pressure the federal government to pass civil rights legislation. Martin Luther King, Jr., gives his most famous speech, "I Have a Dream."
Rosa Parks participates in the March on Washington and is invited to sit on the platform.
Rosa Parks speaks at the SCLC annual conference.
President John F. Kennedy is assassinated in Dallas.

1964   The Mississippi Freedom Summer project begins with the murder of civil rights workers James Chaney, Michael Schwerner, and Andrew Goodman in Philadelphia, Mississippi. The deputy sheriff and six others are prosecuted by the federal government and found guilty of denying the murdered men their civil rights.

Fannie Lou Hamer and others form the Mississippi Freedom Democratic Party (MIFDP) in an attempt to unseat the official white delegation to the 1964 Democratic convention.

Congress passes the Civil Rights Act of 1964. The act bans discrimination in all public accommodations and by employers. It also establishes the Equal Opportunity Employment Commission (EEOC) to monitor compliance with the law.

Dr. Martin Luther King, Jr., receives the Nobel Peace Prize in Stockholm, Sweden.

Rosa Parks attends the ceremony at which the Civil Rights Act is signed into law and becomes a deaconess in Detroit's AME Church.

1965   Malcolm X is assassinated at the Audubon Ballroom in Harlem.

Rosa Parks is one of 600 Alabama civil rights activists who stage a Selma-to-Montgomery protest march. Alabama state police attack the marchers at the Edmund Pettus Bridge. Television stations carry the march and the attack on national television.

President Lyndon Johnson signs the Voting Rights Act into law.

Police arrests in the Watts neighborhood of Los Angeles ignite racial rebellion and riots.

In Detroit, Rosa Parks begins working for Representative John Conyers of Michigan's First District.

1966   Stokely Carmichael is elected to head the SNCC, which calls for Black Power.

Huey Newton, Bobby Seale, and Eldridge Cleaver organize the Black Panther Party for Self-Defense in Oakland, California.

1967   The U.S. Supreme Court, in *Loving v. Virginia*, strikes down state interracial marriage bans.

Major race riots take place in Newark, New Jersey, and Detroit, Michigan.

Thurgood Marshall takes his seat as the first African American justice on the U.S. Supreme Court.

1968   James Earl Ray assassinates Dr. Martin Luther King, Jr., in Memphis, Tennessee. There are 125 cities in 29 states.

Congress enacts the Civil Rights Act of 1968, which outlaws discrimination in the sale and rental of housing.

Sirhan Sirhan assassinates Robert Kennedy in Los Angeles.
Police riots erupt at the Democratic National Convention in
Chicago.

1977   Raymond Parks dies in Detroit.
        On November 27, Sylvester McCauley dies in Detroit.

1978   The U.S. Supreme Court, in *Regents of the University of Cali-
        fornia v. Bakke,* narrowly upholds affirmative action as a legal
        strategy for addressing past discrimination.

1979   Rosa Parks receives the NAACP's Spingarn Medal.
        Rosa Parks's mother, Leona, dies on December 10.

1980   Rosa Parks receives the Martin Luther King, Jr., Award from
        the NAACP.
        The *Detroit News* and Detroit Public Schools establish the
        Rosa Parks Scholarship Foundation.

1983   Rosa Parks is inducted into the Michigan Women's Hall of
        Fame.

1987   Rosa Parks founds the Rosa and Raymond Parks Institute for
        Self-Development.

1988   Rosa Parks retires from her position in the office of Representa-
        tive John Conyers.

1989   Rosa Parks attends the dedication of the Civil Rights Memo-
        rial in Montgomery, Alabama.

1990   Rosa Parks is invited to be part of the welcoming party for Nel-
        son Mandela.

1991   The Smithsonian Institution unveils a bust of Rosa Parks.

1992   Rosa Parks receives the Peace Abbey Courage of Conscience
        Award.

1994   The Rosa Parks Peace Prize is established in Stockholm, Swe-
        den.
        Rosa Parks is attacked in her apartment by Joseph Skipper.

1995   Rosa Parks speaks at the Million Man March.

1996   President Bill Clinton awards the Medal of Freedom to Rosa
        Parks.

1997   Public Act 28 designates the first Monday following February 4
        as Rosa Parks Day in Michigan.

1998   Troy State University at Montgomery, Alabama, opens the
        Rosa Parks Library and Museum on the site of Rosa Parks's ar-
        rest on December 1, 1955.

Rosa Parks opens the Rosa L. Parks Learning Center.

Rosa Parks is inducted into the International Women's Forum Hall of Fame.

Rosa Parks is awarded the International Freedom Conductor Award by the National Underground Railroad Freedom Center.

1999 H.R. Bill 573 passes Congress, awarding Rosa Parks the 121st Congressional Gold Medal.

Rosa Parks is awarded the Detroit-Windsor International Freedom Festival Freedom Award.

Rosa Parks is named by *Time* magazine as one of the 20 most influential figures of the century.

Rosa Parks appears in an episode of the television series *Touched by an Angel*.

Rosa Parks files a lawsuit against the rap group OutKast for using her name without her consent in a song title. The judge rules against Parks, causing public outrage.

2000 Rosa Parks meets with Pope John Paul II in St. Louis and reads a statement asking for racial healing.

Rosa Parks has an audience with the Queen of Swaziland and her children.

Rosa Parks is awarded the Alabama Governor's Medal of Honor.

Rosa Parks is awarded the Alabama Academy Award.

2002 Television movie *The Rosa Parks Story* airs on CBS.

2003 Rosa Parks receives the International Institute Heritage Hall of Fame Award.

2005 At her 92nd birthday celebration at the Calvary Baptist Church, Rosa Parks receives the First Cardinal Dearden Peace Award.

Lawyers for Rosa Parks settle a lawsuit against rap duo OutKast.

Rosa Parks dies on October 24.

Rosa Parks's body lies in state on October 30 and 31 at the U.S. Capitol Rotunda.

2006 A statue of Rosa Parks is placed in National Statuary Hall in Washington, DC.

Chapter 1

THE JOURNEY BEGINS

James McCauley was born in Abbeville, Alabama, a small farm town 95 miles south of Montgomery. McCauley, a skilled carpenter and stonemason, built houses in Alabama's Black Belt region. McCauley met Leona Edwards, a beautiful and proper schoolteacher in Pine Level, Alabama, and the young couple fell in love. They were married on April 12, 1912, in Pine Level's Mount Zion African Methodist Episcopal (AME) Church. Soon after their marriage the McCauleys moved to Tuskegee, the home of Booker T. Washington's Tuskegee Normal Institute, possibly because Tuskegee was known as a model of good race relations and McCauley could find plentiful work building houses in Macon County. Leona found a job teaching. On February 4, 1913, Leona McCauley gave birth to a daughter whom she named Rosa, for her maternal grandmother, Rose Edwards.[1]

Life was not easy for the young family. James traveled throughout Macon County building homes and was often away from home for long stretches of time. Leona had to leave her teaching job until after the baby was born, for at that time school boards did not allow pregnant women to teach. She was often alone in a town where she had no family and knew few people. According to Rosa, her mother often bewailed her predicament, wondering how she was going to manage with a child to care for.[2] Rosa was a small, sickly child, and to make matters even worse for Leona, James's brother Robert moved in with the young family so that he could take courses in carpentry and building at Tuskegee Institute. Despite her loneliness and the added burdens of caring for a second adult, Leona wanted to remain in Tuskegee for the sake of her children. At that time, African Americans believed Tuskegee Institute was the best place in Alabama for blacks to get an education.

Booker T. Washington founded Tuskegee Normal Institute in 1881. Born a slave in Virginia in 1856, Washington overcame poverty through hard work, perseverance, and the help of paternalistic whites. In 1872, Washington arrived at Hampton Institute, a school founded by Samuel Chapman Armstrong and organized around the idea of a "practical education." Armstrong taught his students that "physical work not only increased wage-earning capacity but promoted fidelity, accuracy, honesty, persistence, and intelligence."[3] After completing his education at Hampton Institute, Washington went on to establish Tuskegee Institute, a school based on Armstrong's philosophy of industrial education. As practiced by Armstrong and later Washington, industrial education was a model of black education focused on developing the skills and habits necessary to a dependable, subservient workforce. Over time, Washington became more convinced that his educational philosophy would improve the position of African Americans in the South by not antagonizing whites and carving out an economic place for blacks in their communities. Washington's supporters founded other schools based on his model and designed programs to build character and mold the ideology of prospective teachers. Industrial education glorified the dignity of common labor and celebrated hard work as the means to economic advancement. Advocates organized industrial education around a conservative sociopolitical ideology that discouraged blacks from seeking basic social and political equality.[4] According to historian James Anderson, "'Education for Life' meant training to adjust to a life carved out for blacks within an oppressive social order."[5]

In 1895, Washington delivered an address at the Cotton States Exposition in Atlanta, Georgia, which later became widely known as the Atlanta Compromise. This speech marked Washington's ascendancy among whites as the foremost spokesperson for African Americans.

Washington called on blacks to temporarily accept second-class citizenship, to submit to white social and political rule, and to focus instead on economic advancement and self-help. In this way, Washington claimed, African Americans would eventually acquire property, wealth, and respect. This, along with high moral character, would eventually lead to first-class citizenship and acceptance in white society. To dispel white fears, Washington publicly disapproved of black political participation and renounced agitation and protest for first-class citizenship. African Americans, he argued, must earn citizenship rights. Washington believed that if blacks were humble and submitted to racism, white Americans would realize the wrongs committed against blacks, while the development of high moral character would eliminate white racial animosity.[6]

Washington designed Tuskegee Institute's curriculum to meet his goal of gradual inclusion for African Americans. His plan was to train his students to be teachers, who would then return to their communities and teach moral values, personal hygiene, self-discipline, and the virtues of hard work. In addition to academic and religious training, Tuskegee taught

> thirty-three trades and industries, including carpentry, blacksmithing, printing, wheelwrighting, harnessmaking, painting, machinery, founding, shoemaking, brickmasonry and brickmaking, plastering, sawmilling, tinsmithing, tailoring, mechanical and architectural drawing, electrical and steam engineering, canning, sewing, dressmaking, millinery, cooking, laundering, housekeeping, mattress making, basketry, nursing, agriculture, dairying and stock raising, horticulture.[7]

According to Washington,

> My plan was for them to see not only the utility of labor but its beauty and dignity. They would be taught to lift labor up from drudgery and toil and would learn to love work for its own sake. We wanted them to return to the plantation districts and show people there how to put new energy and new ideas into farming as well as the intellectual and moral and religious life of the people.[8]

At Tuskegee Institute, Washington urged his students to develop the habits and skills—good farm management, thrift, patience, perseverance, high morals, and good manners—that would win them an economic and eventually a social and political place in southern society.

According to Washington, the greatest need for the black man at that point in time was to prepare for the "opportunities of freedom."[9] Many whites, northerners and southerners alike, liked what they saw as Washington's formula for economic and social equilibrium in between the races and his relative disinterest in political and civil rights for blacks. Most whites did not appreciate that Washington's public pronouncements merely indicated that because blacks were starting with so little, they would have to work their way up to positions of power and respectability. They overlooked the implicit assumption of eventual acceptance and integration in Washington's message. On one occasion Washington said,

> I would set no limits to the attainments of the Negro in arts, in letters or statesmanship, but I believe the surest way to reach those ends is by laying the foundation in the little things of life that lie immediately about one's door. I plead for industrial education and development for the Negro not because I want to cramp him, but because I want to free him.[10]

Few whites recognized the expectation of full entrance into the professions, and they did not seem to notice that Washington sent his children to college.

Of course, not all African Americans agreed with Washington's approach to the "race problem." William Monroe Trotter, a militant activist as well as the owner and editor of *The Guardian* of Boston, adamantly opposed Washington's program. W.E.B. Du Bois, a noted black scholar, editor, and civil rights activist, initially supported Washington and agreed with him on strategies for racial advancement that focused on racial solidarity and economic development. However, after Du Bois witnessed racial violence in the South and documented an increasing number of violent assaults against blacks, he questioned Washington's approach. By the early 1900s, Du Bois and Washington publicly disagreed over philosophies, strategies, and leadership.

Du Bois's first public challenge to Washington's leadership was his publication of *The Souls of Black Folk*. In a chapter entitled "Of Mr. Booker T. Washington and Others," Du Bois criticized Washington for compromising with whites at the expense of blacks. Du Bois applauded Washington for encouraging interracial cooperation in the South, inspiring thrift, practical education, and the acquisition of property. However, Du Bois opposed Washington's program when he observed increasing black disenfranchisement, the decline of public school education and the black college, and the reinforced implementation of a color caste system.[11] Du Bois forcefully argued that Washington's racial philosophy was actually promoting racial dehumanization and leading the race backward.

Nevertheless, Leona was very impressed by Booker T. Washington and "admired his ability." She was particularly impressed by Washington's notions that high moral character and absolute cleanliness were "civilizing agents" that would help African Americans advance in American society. Washington's 1901 autobiography *Up from Slavery* held a prominent place in the McCauley household, and Leona McCauley embraced the ideas of Washington's self-help philosophy.[12]

Since James was an excellent carpenter and stonemason, Leona hoped that Tuskegee would hire him to teach carpentry and stonemasonry, which would provide stability for the young family. A teaching position at Tuskegee offered a steady income, housing, and a chance for a good education for their children. James, however, wanted to do contracting work because it paid more money—at least it did until a boll weevil infestation attacked the region's cotton crops and devastated the farm economy. As the region's economy declined, James found less work. Therefore, when Rosa was two years old, James decided that the family should leave Tuskegee and live with his family in Abbeville.[13]

James McCauley's large extended family lived in a small, cramped house. Leona found it difficult to adapt to the overcrowded conditions and did not have a good relationship with her in-laws, so when James decided to go north to find work, Leona, now pregnant with her second child, and Rosa moved in with Leona's parents, Sylvester and Rose Edwards, in Pine Level. When James returned from the north he joined his family, but he left when Rosa was two and a half years old. After that, Rosa recalled, her father did not return until she was five years old and her brother was three. After a few days, he left once again in search of work. Thereafter she did not see James for many years, until after her marriage.[14] According to U.S. Census records, by 1920 James and Leona McCauley had divorced, and Leona married Jim Carlie in 1922.[15]

After Rosa's brother, Sylvester, was born, in August of 1915, Leona went back to teaching. Rosa recalled that her mother went to teach in the village of Spring Hill, since there already was a teacher at the school in Pine Level. Because Spring Hill was far enough from home that Leona could not walk back and forth to the school every day and still adequately prepare her lessons, Leona lived with a family in Spring Hill during the school week.[16] Thus, while Leona earned money to support herself and her children, Rosa's grandparents raised her and her brother. Rosa seemed to enjoy her time in Pine Level with her grandparents and learned a great deal about her family history. Rosa's maternal great-grandfather, James Percival, immigrated to Charleston, South Carolina, from Ireland and married Mary Jane Nobles, a black woman. Their oldest daughter, Rose, was Rosa's grandmother. Her grandfather Sylvester's father was John Edwards, a white plantation owner, and his mother was Edwards's slave. After the death of his mother and John Edwards, the plantation overseer began to abuse Sylvester, and Sylvester developed an "intense and passionate hatred for white people" because of this treatment. According to Rosa, it was her grandfather who instilled in members of the family, from their childhood, the idea that they should not accept mistreatment from anyone: "It was passed down almost in our genes."[17]

Sylvester Edwards's words certainly laid a part of the foundation for Rosa's later actions, but it was most likely his deeds that most influenced her. Sylvester had straight hair and a light complexion and sometimes passed as white. He took advantage of the opportunities this circumstance offered to place whites in situations that they would find unsettling or awkward.[18] When Sylvester met a white person who did not know him, he would extend his hand and shake hands, saying "Edwards is my name."[19] At that time, no white man would shake hands with a black man, and no black man was supposed to introduce himself using his last name. Whites referred to black men by their first names only, or called them "boy" if they were young or "uncle" if they were older. To do otherwise assumed equality between the races, so Sylvester's actions expressed defiance and could have resulted in his lynching or at the very least a whipping. Indeed, mobs had lynched other black men for such "insolent behavior" as refusing to step off a sidewalk to let whites pass or looking whites in the eye. The defiance of segregation laws carried a heavy price.

Sylvester Edwards would not let his grandchildren play with white children either. Rosa remembered that anytime white children in the area wanted to play with Rosa and her brother or Rosa wanted to play with the white children, Edwards would become very hostile. There is no doubt that Edwards was trying to protect his grandchildren; it was not uncommon for white children to call black children "niggers" and taunt them even during play. Edwards was shielding his grandchildren, keeping them away from situations that could damage their self-esteem or result in a physical attack against them. Rosa recalled that her grandfather always looked for ways, however insignificant, of demonstrating his animus against whites.[20] Edwards's obvious defiance of Jim Crow etiquette, his openly belligerent attitude, and his proclivity to laugh at whites behind their backs gave Rosa her first glimpse of overt civil disobedience against discrimination.

Sylvester Edwards protected his family from physical violence as well. The United States has a brutal history of racial violence. At the end of the 19th and beginning of the 20th centuries, lynching became an institutionalized method used by whites to terrorize blacks and maintain white supremacy.

The causes assigned by whites in justification or explanation of lynching Black people include everything from major crimes to minor offenses. In many cases, Blacks were lynched for no reason at all other than race prejudice. Southern folk tradition has held that Negroes were lynched only for the crimes of raping white women—"the nameless crime"—and murder. However, the statistics do not sustain this impression.

The accusations against persons lynched, according to the Tuskegee Institute records for the years 1882 to 1951, were: in 41 per cent for felonious assault, 19.2 per cent for rape, 6.1 per cent for attempted rape, 4.9 per cent for robbery and theft, 1.8 per cent for

insult to white persons, and 22.7 per cent for miscellaneous offenses or no offense at all. In the last category are all sorts of trivial
"offenses" such as "disputing with a white man," attempting to
register to vote, "unpopularity," self-defense, testifying against a
white man, "asking a white woman in marriage," and "peeping in
a window."[21]

Between 1900 and 1920, a reported 1,413 African Americans became
victims of lynching.[22] Lynching became commonplace in the early 20th
century, thanks in part to the resurgence of the Ku Klux Klan (KKK).
Disaffected ex-Confederate soldiers began the Ku Klux Klan in Pulaski,
Tennessee, in 1866. By 1872, the KKK officially disbanded after the
federal government passed the Ku Klux Klan Act, also called the Civil
Rights Act of 1871 or the Force Act of 1871,[23] intended to protect African Americans from violence perpetrated by the KKK. In 1915, William Simmons, an itinerant minister, organized a new KKK in Stone
Mountain, Georgia, inspired in part by the favorable portrayal of the
KKK in D. W. Griffith's epic film, *The Birth of a Nation*. Emphasizing
costumes, rallies, and secret rituals, the new KKK grew rapidly, becoming a national organization and spreading to the North and West. The
new KKK did not focus its attention only on African Americans; this
second incarnation of the Klan was anti-immigrant, anti-Catholic, and
anti-Jew as well. Klan members feared the rapid changes taking place
in America's economy and society. Some Americans perceived rapid
industrialization, increased immigration, and increasing urbanization
as a threat to America's traditional values and way of life. The KKK appealed to these fears of a declining "American civilization" by touting
the organization's goal of 100 percent Americanism; at its peak in the
mid-1920s, the new KKK achieved a total membership of four million
or more. Members served in state legislatures and Congress, and voters
elected KKK members to the governorship in several states. Indiana,
Oklahoma, Texas, and Oregon saw significant KKK influence.[24]

Another reason for the increase in KKK activity was that African
American soldiers were returning from World War I and openly refusing
to abide by segregation laws. These black men had just finished fighting
a war "to make the world safe for democracy." More than 2,290,525 African American men registered for service and some 367,000 served in

the military.[25] These veterans had served their country, fought bravely, and were highly decorated. They had experienced racial harmony in the trenches of France and been welcomed by the French people as equals. They moved around freely in France and associated openly with French men and women. The French welcomed black soldiers into their homes and tried to make them comfortable. Many white soldiers resented the fact that the French were instilling the expectation of equal treatment among African American soldiers. Some white soldiers warned the French that they should not treat blacks with common civility; that African American men were wanton rapists whose innate depravity compelled white Americans to lynch them so as to protect white society. Hearing rumors of black men raping French women, the secretary of war sent Robert Moton, Booker T. Washington's successor at Tuskegee, to France to look into the matter and speak to the black soldiers. After investigating the allegations, Moton found that charges against black soldiers were few and convictions even fewer. Nevertheless, he warned the black soldiers that they should not expect the kind of freedom in America that they had enjoyed in France. Moton told the men that they would have to remain content with the same position they had always held in the United States.[26] African American veterans, however, wanted America to live up to its professed values of freedom and equality for all.

Some whites did not like that attitude, so the KKK grew and violence against African Americans increased, perpetuated by those both inside and outside the Klan. White vigilantes lynched more than 70 blacks between 1918 and 1919. Ten black soldiers, still in uniform, died when white mobs attacked them. In Mississippi and Georgia, mobs murdered three black veterans. Vigilantes in Arkansas lynched two veterans, Florida and Alabama mobs murdered one black veteran each. White mobs burned 11 of 14 black men while still alive. James Weldon Johnson called the summer of 1919 the Red Summer because of the level of violence against blacks. From June until December there were about twenty-five race riots across America, from Longview, Texas, to Chicago and to Rosewood, Florida. White vigilante groups across America, in both the North and South, used organized violence to deprive blacks of some of the gains they had made during the war. African Americans fought back, the black press decried the violence, and the NAACP lobbied Congress for an antilynching bill, all to no avail. Nevertheless, African Americans continued to resist and demand equality. World War I had raised the hopes of blacks in America; most African Americans hoped that they would see a new era of opportunity in employment and civil rights. More importantly, they were willing to fight for opportunity and equality as never before.

Rosa remembered that by 1918, when she was six, she had come to understand that blacks were "actually not free."[27] She recalled how her grandfather responded to the KKK parading up and down the road in front of the Edwards home:

> At one point the violence was so bad that my grandfather kept his gun—a double barreled shot gun—close by at all times. And I remember we talked about how just in case the Klansmen broke into our house, we should go to bed with our clothes on so we would be ready to run if we had to. I remember my grandfather saying, "I don't know how long I would last if they came breaking in here, but I'm getting the first one who comes through the door."[28]

Sylvester Edwards was not looking for trouble, but if it found him, he was ready to respond and do his best to protect his family. Rosa learned something from her grandfather's behavior and words; self-defense was an acceptable use of violence, and the Christian admonition to "turn the other cheek" did not apply when one's life was at stake.

The Edwardses were the only African American family to own land in their vicinity. They owned 18 acres, on which they had fruit and nut trees and a vegetable garden; they also raised chickens and cows. Sylvester sold or traded eggs, chickens, and calves at local stores for whatever the family needed because they earned very little money from working on other farms and from Leona's teaching. When the Edwards family finished with working their own land, they worked nearby, picking cotton for Moses Hudson. By the time she was seven years old, Rosa was taken to the fields, given an empty flour sack, and expected to pick one or two pounds of cotton per day. As she grew older, she picked and chopped the weeds in Hudson's cotton fields. Chopping paid 50 cents per day while picking paid a dollar for every 100 pounds picked. Rosa remembered working "from can to can't," meaning from when you can see (sunup) to when you can't (sundown).[29]

Later Rosa would recall that she was aware of big differences between blacks and whites by the time she began school. The black school was inferior to the white school. Black children went to a one-teacher, one-room schoolhouse located in the yard of the Mount Zion AME Church. The school included grades one through six, with about 60 students, and the school year was five months long. When the weather turned cold, the older boys would go out and cut wood to heat the schoolhouse, or sometimes a parent would come by with a wagon full of wood. Rosa remembered that the white children had a new brick school building paid for by the taxpayers and the town or county took care of heating the building. White children had a separate classroom for each grade level and attended school for nine months each year. Even though the white school was closer to her home, Rosa and the other black children walked to school while the white children rode a school bus. Sometimes the white children on the school buses would pass the black children walking to school and throw trash at them; therefore the black children would move off the road and walk in the fields a short distance away whenever they saw the school bus coming.[30] At that time, African Americans had very few options for protest; for many, life was a struggle for dignity and survival.

These circumstances dictated that Rosa should learn to protect herself. When she was about 10 years old, a white boy named Franklin said something offensive to her and threatened to hit her. She picked up a brick and dared him to hit her. Franklin decided to go away and leave Rosa alone. When she told her grandmother about the incident, Rose reprimanded Rosa. Rose told her granddaughter that she had to learn how to deal with whites. Retaliation was not an option. Grandmother Rose's words upset her, although later she realized that her grandmother was afraid for her.[31] In another instance, a white boy on roller skates tried to slam into Rosa and knock her off a sidewalk. She turned around and pushed him. His mother was nearby and saw what had happened. She threatened to have Rosa arrested and jailed for pushing her son, to which Rosa defiantly replied that he pushed her first even though she was not bothering him.[32] Rosa had a defiant streak and a strong sense of what was fair. She took her grandfather's lessons to heart: African Americans had the right to defend themselves. A white teacher in Montgomery, Alabama, would reinforce that idea and introduce Rosa McCauley to the world beyond Pine Level.

NOTES

1. Rosa Parks with Jim Haskins, *Rosa Parks: My Story* (New York: Puffin Books, 1992), 4–6; Douglas Brinkley, *Rosa Parks; A Life* (New York: Penguin Books, 2000), 11–15.

2. Rosa Parks, *My Story* (New York: Penguin Books, 1992), 6.

3. John Hope Franklin and Alfred A. Moss, *From Slavery to Freedom*, 8th ed. (New York: McGraw Hill, 2000), 299.

4. See Carter G. Woodson, *The Mis-education of the Negro* (Washington, DC: Associated Publishers, 1969); Donald Spivey, *Schooling for the New Slavery: Black Industrial Education, 1868–1915* (Westport, CT: Greenwood Press, 1978), 79; Henry S. Enck, "Black Self-Help in the Progressive Era: The 'Northern Campaigns' of Smaller Southern Black Industrial Schools, 1900–1915," *Journal of Negro History* 61, 1 (January 1976): 79–80.

5. James Anderson, *Education of Blacks in the South, 1860–1935* (Chapel Hill: University of North Carolina Press, 1988), 57.

6. Booker T. Washington, "Industrial Education for the Negro," in *The Negro Problem* (New York: James Potts and Company, 1903); see also Louis R. Harlan, *Booker T. Washington:* vol. 1, *The Making of a Black Leader, 1856–1901* (New York: Oxford University Press, 1975); and *Booker T. Washington:* vol. 2, *The Wizard Of Tuskegee, 1901–1915* (New York: Oxford University Press, 1983).

7. Washington, "Industrial Education for the Negro."

8. *The Rise and Fall of Jim Crow*, http://www.pbs.org/wnet/jimcrow/stories_events_tuskegee.html (accessed June 25, 2009).

9. Booker T. Washington, "Chapters from My Experience," *World's Work* 21 (November 1910).

10. Franklin and Moss, *From Slavery to Freedom*, 303.

11. W.E.B. Du Bois, *The Souls of Black Folk* (New York: Oxford University Press, Reprint, 2009), 94.

12. Brinkley, *Rosa Parks*, 18.

13. Parks, *My Story*, 7–8.

14. Ibid., 9–10.

15. "Ancestors of Rosa (McCauley) Parks," ProGenealogists, http://www.progenealogists.com/parks/aqwg01.htm#1 (accessed June 25, 2009).

16. Parks, My Story, 19.

17. Ibid., 14–15.

18. Ibid., 15.

19. Ibid., 16.

20. Ibid., 17.

21. Robert A. Gibson, "The Negro Holocaust: Lynching and Race Riots in the United States, 1880–1950," Yale–New Haven Teachers Institute, http://www.yale.edu/ynhti/curriculum/units/1979/2/79.02.04.x.html (accessed June 25, 2009).

22. Gibson, "The Negro Holocaust."

23. Ku Klux Klan Act, http://law.jrank.org/pages/8020/Ku-Klux-Klan-Act.html (accessed June 29, 2009).

24. David H. Chalmers, Hooded Americanism: The History of the Ku Klux Klan, 3rd ed. (Chapel Hill, NC: Duke University Press, 1987); Nancy K. MacLean, Behind the Mask of Chivalry: The Making of the Second Ku Klux Klan (New York: Oxford University Press, 1995); David A. Horowitz, Inside the Klavern: The Secret History of a Ku Klux Klan of the 1920s (Carbondale, IL: Southern Illinois University Press, 1999).

25. Franklin and Moss, From Slavery to Freedom, 360.

26. Ibid., 373.

27. Parks, My Story, 30.

28. Ibid.

29. Ibid., 33–35.

30. Ibid., 24–29.

31. Ibid., 22–23.

32. Brinkley, Rosa Parks, 28.

Chapter 2

COMING OF AGE IN MONTGOMERY

When Rosa was eight years old, she traveled to Montgomery, Alabama, with Leona, who was attending Alabama State Normal College, taking summer classes to keep her teaching certificate current. Since Jim Crow segregation dictated that African Americans could not stay in hotels or white boarding houses, Rosa and Leona lived with her grandmother's first cousin, Ida Nobles. Leona thought this was an ideal situation. Over the summer, Rosa and Cousin Ida could get to know each other and, in the fall, Rosa could stay in Montgomery to attend school there. Leona wanted to enroll Rosa in school in Montgomery because the school term was nine months long instead of only five, as in Pine Level. Cousin Ida also lived next door to a doctor and Rosa suffered from chronic tonsillitis, so medical help would be nearby. Cousin Ida loved Rosa, but she did not want Rosa to simply stay with her, she wanted to adopt her legally. Leona would not hear of that, so she and Rosa moved in with another cousin, Cousin Lelar. During that summer, Rosa attended a laboratory school at Alabama State Normal College, where student teachers gained valuable experience teaching the children of the summer students. When Leona finished her classes, she and Rosa returned to Pine Level.[1]

Leona's decision to have her child live with a relative so as to attend
a school far from home was not uncommon among African American
families at the time. Local school boards in rural areas were often poorly
funded, leading to overcrowded and inadequately supplied classrooms.
Many rural teachers were poorly educated themselves. African Americans innately understood the connection between education and freedom, and families often sacrificed to make sure that their children were
well educated. In some cases, entire communities pitched in to send a
child to a better school. In 1924, when Rosa was 11 years old, she had
her tonsils removed in Montgomery, and she became much healthier
than she had been as a small child.[2] After recovering from the operation, Rosa moved in with her Aunt Fannie Williamson, a widow with
four children, and Leona enrolled her at the Montgomery Industrial
School for Girls. Cofounded in 1866 by Alice L. White and H. Margaret
Beard, this school offered elementary education, kindergarten through
eighth grade, to 325 African American girls. Ten white teachers instructed the students in both literary and industrial subjects, including English, science, and geography, although the curriculum focused
on industrial courses, including cooking, sewing, nurse's training, and
practical classes in hygiene and care of the sick.[3] One visitor wrote:

The Montgomery Industrial School is a good example of the
value of such schools not only to the negro population, but also
to the white community. I witnessed a primary lesson in domestic
science in which the girls were instructed that when they came
into the kitchen to prepare a meal their hands, their nails, their
aprons, and every utensil must be scrupulously clean; that every
article of food must be carefully guarded against the slightest con-
tamination or infection, and that their task must be performed
with conscientious fidelity. This spirit runs through all the work
of the school. These girls, after being trained, go into the white
families of Montgomery to cook the food, take care of sleeping
apartments, and nurse children. The careful training which they
receive becomes a direct contribution to the comfort, health and
safety of their white neighbors, while the training which they
have received in morals and conscientious industry greatly in-
creases their efficiency.[4]

The curriculum at the Montgomery Industrial School closely followed the pragmatic approach inspired by Booker T. Washington at Tuskegee Institute, and Washington supported White's educational strategy. In a fundraising letter for the school, Washington wrote, "I have kept up with the work that Misses White and Beard are doing in Montgomery, Alabama, Industrial School, and have no hesitation in saying that they are doing good, practical work in that city."[5] He went on to praise White and Beard for connecting the work done in the classroom to the home and for spending the funds they received wisely.

White's school also reinforced strict Christian morality. Each day the students listened to some part of the New Testament, and prayers were an important part of every class. Rosa was already a devout child, and under White's care she became, in the words of her childhood friend Johnnie Mae Carr, "a straight Christian arrow."[6] White did not allow dancing, racy music, lipstick, or hoop earrings; she did not allow her students to go to the movies. Rosa remembered White as "a very strict disciplinarian, she always saw to it that the girls were not liars, or that they dressed neatly, wore no jewelry. She frowned on—we called it bobbed hair—cutting the hair and so on."[7]

Rosa remembered that Leona paid tuition at the school when she first enrolled her daughter there, but later Rosa became a scholarship student. This arrangement was similar to work–study today. As a scholarship student, Rosa was required to clean two classrooms after school, including sweeping, dusting, emptying wastebaskets, and cleaning the blackboards. After completing these tasks, Rosa walked to Aunt Fannie's, where she would have general chores to do before getting her school uniform washed and cleaned for the next day. Although there was little time for leisure activities, Rosa looked back on this time as laying the foundation for her civil rights activism.

What I learned best at Miss White's school was that I was a person with dignity and self-respect, and I should not set my sights lower than anybody else just because I was black. We were taught to be ambitious and to believe that we could do what we wanted in life.[8]

Miss White and the teachers at the Montgomery Industrial School reinforced the lessons Rosa learned from her family in Pine Level. Although the school closed after Rosa completed the eighth grade, she continued her education at the Booker T. Washington Junior High School and then attended the laboratory school at Alabama Normal School during her junior year of high school, since there were no public high schools for blacks in Montgomery until 1938. After about a month, Rosa dropped out of the 11th grade and returned to Pine Level to care for her grandmother, who was ill. After her grandmother's death, Rosa returned to Montgomery and took her first job in a factory that made blue denim work shirts. She went back to school at Alabama State for a short time, but had to drop out a second time to care for Leona, who suffered from migraine headaches and swelling of the legs and feet. Although Rosa regretted leaving school on both occasions, she considered it her responsibility to take care of her grandmother and later her mother without complaint, saying that "it was just something that had to be done."[9]

Despite the valuable foundation of self-esteem built at the Montgomery Industrial School, Rosa's experiences in Montgomery were not all positive. Jim Crow segregation and racism were more obvious in the city than in the relatively protected environment of Pine Level, and Rosa experienced it at first hand. Montgomery segregated its streetcars, and although blacks tried to avoid using them as much as possible, they rode them when the weather was bad. Black passengers were compelled to move as far to the back of the streetcars as they could. Public water fountains had signs marked "White" and "Colored." Rosa recalled that as a child she "wondered if 'White' water tasted different from 'Colored' water and if 'Colored' water came in different colors."[10] One day when Rosa and her cousin Annie Mae were picking berries in a vacant lot, a white boy called the girls niggers and demanded that they leave the berries alone. Rosa and Annie Mae told him to leave them alone or they would hit him. Later, when they told Aunt Fannie about the incident, she castigated the girls. Aunt Fannie was afraid for the girls. Even though the incident was a simple childhood altercation, Aunt Fannie knew that if the white boy had told someone about the girls' words, whites could lynch them and the family would be able to do nothing to protect them. There were other run-ins with white children, but Rosa believed that the white children were not naturally cruel; rather, she felt that they had absorbed the attitudes of the adults they lived among.[11]

Rosa McCauley spent the next several years caring for her mother, cleaning white people's homes, and taking in sewing. She was a faithful, dedicated member of St. Paul AME Church, where she found spiritual comfort and joy and once served as Sunday school superintendent.[12] Rosa enjoyed attending church services; she especially enjoyed the hymns and learning about the history of the AME Church.[13] For Rosa and many other African American women, the church served as a special place; it represented a refuge from the racism and discrimination that beleaguered them daily. It was a place where African American women could gather and share their trials, build their faith, and renew their strength. It was a place of spiritual guidance, "which provides recreation and relaxation...a place which shelters the community feeling; enables escape from the hard and negative life experiences; holds together families."[14] Rosa had a deeply rooted faith, believing that God had given her the courage to speak up for what was right. According to Douglas Brinkley, "faith in God was never the question for Rosa Parks; it was the answer."[15] Rosa's faith in God sustained her, but when she fell in love with Raymond Parks, her political activism was born.

Raymond Parks was born on February 12, 1903, in Wedowee, Alabama, northeast of Montgomery. When Raymond was just an infant, his father, David Parks, who worked as a carpenter, fell off a roof and died. His mother, Gerri Culbertson Parks, taught him to read and write, but she died when he was in his teens. Raymond, so light-skinned that he could be mistaken for white, grew up as the only black child in an all-white neighborhood. Aside from his mother's home schooling, he had little formal education, having attended school only briefly in Roanoke, Alabama, where he worked as a sexton at a white Baptist church.[16] After an altercation over watering shrubbery at the church, Raymond headed to Tuskegee, where he learned to cut hair and became a barber. At 28 years of age, he moved to Montgomery, where he found work at O. L. Campbell's barbershop.[17] It was here that he first met Rosa McCauley.

First introduced to Raymond by a mutual friend, Rosa was uninterested because Raymond had just ended a relationship and she, too, had

"had some unhappy romantic experiences." In addition, Rosa recalled her impression that "He was too white."[18] Undeterred, Raymond appeared at Rosa's home in a shiny red Nash, offering to take her out for a Sunday afternoon ride. Before long, Rosa decided that Raymond was not only a very nice man but also interesting and intelligent, and she enjoyed talking to him. She was pleased that he "didn't seem to have that meek attitude—what we call an 'Uncle Tom' attitude—toward white people."[19] Raymond Parks was the first man Rosa ever talked to about the racial situation in the South.[20] The more she learned about him, the more she began to respect and love him. In December 1932, Rosa McCauley and Raymond Parks were married in a simple ceremony in Pine Level, Alabama.[21]

Raymond introduced Rosa to political activism through his activities in the NAACP. By 1932, the NAACP had a long history of fighting against segregation. Mary White Ovington, one of the original founders of the NAACP, explained the origins of the NAACP and the motivations for the founding in a history written in 1914. Ovington was born on April 11, 1865, three days before President Abraham Lincoln's assassination, in Brooklyn, New York. Ovington's upbringing in an upper-class home, her abolitionist parents, her Unitarian religious beliefs, and her studies at the Harvard Annex (later called Radcliffe College) helped to shape her beliefs about the origin of social problems. In the 1890s, Ovington joined the settlement house movement, where she worked to eliminate child labor and tenement sweatshops through legislation and public education. After hearing Booker T. Washington speak in Boston in 1903, Ovington became aware of racial discrimination in the North, and from this point on, she would make the achievement of racial equality her life's goal. By 1904, she had begun a study of housing and employment problems among New York's black population and in 1911 published *Half a Man: The Status of the Negro in New York*. In 1908—after the outbreak of race riots in Springfield, Illinois, the home of Abraham Lincoln—she joined forces with American socialist and reformer William English Walling.

According to the official history of the riot,

On August 14, 1908, tension filled the air as two black men sat in the county jail, accused of unrelated sexual assault and murder crimes against whites. A large white crowd had gathered outside the jail, wanting to take matters in their own hands, chanting for vigilante justice.

Sensing the imminent danger for the two prisoners, police secretly took them out through the back door and put them on a train to a jail 60 miles away. After they learned that the police tricked them and the prisoners were gone, the angry mob erupted in violence, destroying buildings, looting, and eventually lynching two prominent members of the black community. The rampage continued until Governor Charles Deneen called in the Illinois National Guard to control the situation.[22]

After reading Walling's article about the riot entitled "Race War in the North," Ovington, Walling, and Dr. Henry Moscowitz, a reformer with a broad knowledge of conditions among New York's immigrants, met in a little New York apartment to discuss how they could overcome racial violence and discrimination. For two years, the fledgling organization held annual conferences inviting the most prominent social reformers of the day. The NAACP, as we know it today, was officially

Attorney Samuel Leibowitz meets with four of the nine Scottsboro Boys in his New York City office on July 26, 1937, two days after charges against these four were dropped. Left to right, Willie Roberson, Eugene Williams, Leibowitz, Roy Wright, and Olen Montgomery. (AP Photo)

founded by a multiracial group of activists, including Ida Wells-Barnett, W.E.B. Du Bois, Moscowitz, Ovington, Oswald Garrison Villard, and Walling on February 12, 1909. The primary goal of the association was to renew the struggle to gain civil and political liberty for African Americans.[23] It was at the second conference that W.E.B. Du Bois, then at Atlanta University, joined the organization. Writing the first official history of the association in 1914, Ovington recorded,

> When Dr. DuBois came to us we were brought closely in touch with an organization of colored people, formed in 1905 at Niagara and known as the Niagara Movement. This organization had held important conferences at Niagara, Harpers Ferry, and Boston, and had attempted a work of legal redress along very much the lines upon which the National Association for the Advancement of Colored People was working.[24]

Just four years after the founding of the national association, the NAACP became the leading advocate for black constitutional rights in Alabama. Other organizations existed, such as civic and voters' leagues, but the NAACP provided the most constant and visible challenge to African Americans' second-class status in society. White supremacists viewed the NAACP as a threat to the status quo and used intimidation, violence, and the law in their attempts to eliminate the various branches in the state. As a charter member of the Montgomery Chapter of the NAACP, Raymond Parks put himself at great risk, but the black community respected him for his activism. His barbershop became a center for the distribution for "race papers." He made sure that the NAACP's journal *The Crisis* was on hand for his customers along with the major black newspapers of the time, including the *Pittsburgh Courier, Amsterdam News,* and *Chicago Defender.* However, Raymond's all-consuming passion was the case of the Scottsboro Boys. Rosa recalled that "It gnawed at him to see those innocent kids were framed. He'd say, 'I'll never sleep until they're free.'"[25] The case was a cause célèbre of the 1930s. For white southerners, the case was about racial insubordination; for African Americans it reflected nearly 300 years of exploitation and abuse suffered at the hands of white America.

During the Great Depression, many young people took to the road, hoboing across the nation in rail cars in search of work. On March 25, 1931, about two dozen young black and white men and a few young women rode the Southern Railroad's Chattanooga-to-Memphis freight cars in search of jobs in Memphis. Soon after the train crossed the Alabama border, one of the white youths stepped on the hand of one of the black youths while walking across the top of a tank car. A stone throwing fight erupted between the white and black teenagers and eventually the black youths forced all but one of the white teenagers off the train. Some of the white teenagers then went to the stationmaster in Stevenson, Alabama, to report an "assault" by a gang of blacks. The stationmaster wired ahead to Paint Rock, the next station, and a posse met the train. The armed posse arrested nine black teenagers for assaulting the white teenagers, tied them together with a plow line, loaded them on a flatbed truck, and took them to jail in Scottsboro, Alabama.[26]

The posse also removed two white women, Victoria Price and Ruby Bates, who had been working as prostitutes from the train. The women then accused the black youths of gang rape. The posse took the women to the jail, where Victoria Price identified six of the nine black teenagers as the men who raped her. The guard reportedly then said, "If those six had Miss Price, it stands to reason that the others had Miss Bates."[27] In the meantime, a crowd of several hundred white men gathered outside the jail hoping to lynch the young men. However, Governor B. M. Miller ordered the Alabama National Guard to protect the suspects. Twelve days later, the Scottsboro Boys, as the young men had become known, went to trial in Judge A. E. Hawkins's courtroom. Before the trial even began, local newspaper reports had already convicted the young men. In addition, the defense attorneys were clearly incompetent. They allowed the prosecution to try the teenagers in groups of two or three, had few questions on cross examination for Victoria Price, did not question the inconsistencies between the testimony of Price and Bates, and did not ask any questions of the physicians who examined Price and Bates.

> The defense offered only the defendants themselves as witnesses, and their testimony was rambling, sometimes incoherent, and riddled with obvious misstatements. Six of the boys (Andy Wright,

Willie Roberson, Charles Weems, Ozie Powell, Olen Montgomery, and Eugene Williams) denied raping or even having seen the two girls. But three others, all who later claimed they did so because of beatings and threats, said that a gang rape by other defendants did occur. Clarence Norris provided what one paper called "the highlight of the trial" when he said of the other blacks, "They all raped her, everyone of them." No closing argument was offered by defense attorneys. A local editorialist described the state's case as "so conclusive as to be almost perfect."[28]

When the trials were over, the juries had found eight of the nine Scottsboro Boys guilty and sentenced them to death. A hung jury resulted in a mistrial for 12-year-old Roy Wright.[29]

The harsh sentences mobilized public opinion, and after a series of appeals, the U.S. Supreme Court, in 1932, overturned the convictions, ruling that the accused had not had adequate legal counsel. The state of Alabama immediately began a second trial, and attorney Samuel Leibowitz, hired by the Communist-sponsored International Labor Defense, argued the Scottsboro Boys' case. During this second trial, doctors testified that Victoria Price and Ruby Bates had lied about the rapes, and Bates testified that the rapes never occurred. Nevertheless, the jury found the young men guilty. For the next five years, both state and federal courts plea-bargained the deal and finally struck a compromise in 1937. This freed four of the nine black men and sentenced the others to lengthy prison terms for a crime that never occurred. The last defendant was finally released on parole in 1950.[30]

According to historian Douglas Brinkley, during the trial the local newspaper in Montgomery, the *Montgomery Advertiser*, immediately labeled the Scottsboro Boys rapists and police began to arrest African Americans on suspicion of being Communists. Raymond Parks began a legal defense fund to help the young men pay their lawyers and avoid the electric chair.[31] He attended regular late-night meetings about the Scottsboro case but refused to let Rosa attend because of the danger. He also refused to tell her what went on at the meetings, so that if she were ever questioned she could truthfully say that she did not know anything. Raymond did hold one meeting at their home, however. Rosa remembered that the men sat around a small table and she was taken aback by the number of guns in the room: "The table was covered with guns." Rosa sat on the back porch with her head on her knees. After the meeting, Raymond took her by the shoulders and brought her inside the house. Rosa recalled that she was shaken and profoundly depressed to see that for black men, simply holding a meeting might result in injury or death.[32] The police were on the lookout for these meeting places and openly used fear and intimidation against blacks to stop their activities. Nevertheless, Rosa was proud of Raymond's efforts on behalf of the Scottsboro Boys, admiring his courage in face of the risks he was taking. Over time, she wrote, she found that he was dedicated to bettering life for his race and his family as well as for himself.[33] Raymond's activism was no small feat. The 1930s were dangerous times for southern black activists. During the Great Depression, white supremacists took all challenges to racial segregation very seriously, and membership in the NAACP was indistinguishable from treason in their eyes.

While Raymond fought for the Scottsboro Boys and tried to protect Rosa from any repercussions due to his activities, he also encouraged her to return to school to complete her high school education. In 1933, at the age of 20, Rosa Parks earned her high school diploma. This may seem like a small step by today's standards, just the first step on the way to a college degree. But for African Americans in the 1930s, a high school diploma was a major achievement. Very few African Americans had the chance to attend high school. In fact, by the mid-1930s in the southern states, "eight out of every ten black children of high school age were not enrolled in secondary schools."[34] In 1940 in the states with the highest black populations—Alabama, Arkansas, Georgia, Louisiana, Mississippi, and South Carolina—less than 18 percent of blacks of high school age were enrolled in secondary schools.[35] Rosa herself later commented that even in 1940, seven years after she received her own diploma, only seven out of every hundred high school–aged students managed to graduate from high school.[36] In fact, in 1940 the percentage of African Americans over age 25 in Alabama who had earned a high school diploma was even lower than Rosa Parks reported. According to the U.S. Census Bureau, only 3.9 percent of blacks over age 25 in Alabama held a high school diploma in 1940; nationwide, only 7.7 percent had graduated from high school.[37]

Despite having earned a high school diploma, however, Rosa did not have much success in getting a meaningful job. Because there were government jobs in the state capital, Montgomery's residents suffered less unemployment than people living in other cities in Alabama, but government officials did not hire African Americans for civil service positions. Confined to menial work despite her high school diploma, Rosa worked as a nurse's assistant at St. Margaret's Hospital and took in sewing on the side. In 1941, after the onset of World War II, new employment opportunities opened at Maxwell Field, an Army Air Corps base two miles outside of Montgomery. At that time, President Franklin D. Roosevelt, recognizing the increasing voting power of African Americans, banned racial segregation in public places and on public transportation at U.S. military bases. Rosa began working at Maxwell Field in 1941, and she naturally recognized the stark contrast between the integrated facilities and transportation on the base and the segregation off base. She could ride an integrated trolley at the Army Air Corps base, but off base she still had to confront the indignities of segregated buses in order to return home.[38] She faced the hypocrisy of racial segregation every day; the experience was degrading. Rosa Parks's experiences at Maxwell Field most certainly spurred her to action. According to historian Douglas Brinkley, "It was, in fact, a U.S. military base that showed Rosa Parks, who had never left Alabama, how fair American society could be."[39] Jim Crow segregation looked even more ugly when juxtaposed with the integrated army facilities just two miles outside of Montgomery. Rosa Parks was more determined than ever to do something to end the second-class citizenship of African Americans in Montgomery. And beginning in the 1930s, southern white racial liberals began to join with African Americans to organize new interracial organizations to fight segregation.

One such organization was the Southern Conference for Human Welfare (SCHW), an interracial coalition of southern liberals, intellectuals, labor leaders, and activists dedicated to improving civil liberties, justice, and equality.

The Southern Conference for Human Welfare held its inaugural meeting in Birmingham on November 20, 1938, in the Municipal Auditorium. The attendees consisted of leading southern liberals, including Supreme Court Justice Hugo Black; Aubrey Williams of the Works Progress Administration; Mary McLeod Bethune, James Dombrowski, one of the organizers of the Highlander Folk School; Alabama Governor Bibb Graves; and activist Virginia Foster Durr.[40]

The SCHW drew delegates from throughout the South; they fought for southern industrial development, minimum wage and maximum hours legislation, educational equality, voting rights, the abolition of the poll tax, abolition of tenant and sharecropper systems, and antilynching legislation. The SCHW also opposed segregation and tried to hold nonsegregated meetings in the South, although the race issue was always conspicuous. In fact, on the second day of the conference, Birmingham's police commissioner, Eugene "Bull" Connor, "famously informed attendees that they were forbidden to "segregate together."[41] Reluctantly, the attendees complied with the laws, with whites sitting on one side of the auditorium and about 1,200 African American delegates on the other. In response, First Lady Eleanor Roosevelt, a featured speaker at the convention, placed her chair on the line dividing the auditorium and the delegates and vowed not to hold any future meetings in cities where local laws required segregation. Unfortunately, the leadership steered clear of more sweeping denunciations of Jim Crow segregation. Although the SCHW made little real progress and was constantly under fire for being a Communist-front organization, it "was significant...because it provided one of the earliest interracial public voices against segregation. It was a model of interracial cooperation at a time when Jim Crow was still deeply entrenched in southern culture." For a very brief period, racial liberalism found a voice in southern politics and culture, and the SCHW was one of the most important outlets for southern liberal thought.[42]

Although we do not know if Rosa Parks was aware of the SCHW, its very existence opened new avenues for protest. It was because of the formation of interracial organizations in the 1930s and 1940s that the NAACP could find fertile ground for organizing new chapters throughout the South. These chapters would be instrumental in fighting for voter registration.

NOTES

1. Rosa Parks, *My Story* (New York: Penguin Books, 1992), 40–41.

2. Marcia M. Greenlee, "Interview with Rosa McCauley Parks" on August 22 and 23, 1978, in *The Black Woman Oral History Project*, vol. 8, ed. Ruth Edmonds Hill (Westport, CT: Meckler, 1991), 248.

3. Thomas Jesse Jones, "Negro Education: A Study of the Private and Higher Schools for Colored People in the United States," Phelps-Stokes Fund, vol. 2 (Washington, DC: Government Printing Office, 1917), 77–78.

4. Hastings H. Hart, "Social Problems of Alabama: A Study of the Social Institutions and Agencies of the State of Alabama Made at the Request of Governor Charles Henderson" (New York: Russell Sage Foundation, 1918), 42.

5. Douglas Brinkley, *Rosa Parks; A Life* (New York: Penguin Books, 2000), 29.

6. Ibid., 34.

7. Greenlee, "Interview with Rosa McCauley Parks," 246.

8. Ibid., 247; Parks, *My Story*, 49; Brinkley, *Rosa Parks*, 35.

9. Parks, *My Story*, 53–54.

10. Ibid., 46.

11. Ibid., 51–53.

12. Erica Pippins and Jannell McGrew, "Pomp Sendoff 'What She Deserved,'" *Montgomery Advertiser* (April 6, 2009).

13. Greenlee, "Interview with Rosa McCauley Parks," 249.

14. LaVerne Gyant, "Passing the Torch: African American Women in the Civil Rights Movement," *Journal of Black Studies* 26, no. 5, Special Issue: The Voices of African American Women in the Civil Rights Movement (May 1996): 637.

15. Randall Bush, "Remembering Rosa Parks," *Theological Studies*: 65 (2004): 846–47.

16. Parks, *My Story*, 57.

17. Greenlee, "Interview with Rosa McCauley Parks," 251–52; Brinkley, *Rosa Parks*, 38.

18. Parks, *My Story*, 55.

19. Ibid., 59.

20. Greenlee, "Interview with Rosa McCauley Parks," 252.

21. Ibid., 251.

22. "The Springfield Race Riot of 1908," www.visit-springfieldillinois.com/.../1908-RaceRiot-Brochure.pdf (accessed July 27, 2009).

23. "History of the NAACP," http://www.naacp.org/about/history/timeline/index.htm (accessed July 27, 2009).

24. Mary White Ovington, *The Walls Came Tumbling Down* (New York: Harcourt, Brace and Company; 1st stated edition, 1947); Mary White Ovington and Ralph E. Luker, *Black and White Sat Down Together: The Reminiscences of an NAACP Founder* (New York: The Feminist Press at CUNY, 1996); "History of the NAACP," http://www.naacp.org/about/history/howbegan/index.htm (accessed July 27, 2009).

25. Brinkley, *Rosa Parks*, 39.

26. Dan T. Carter, *Scottsboro: A Tragedy of the American South* (New York: Oxford University Press, 1969); Famous American Trials, http://www.law.umkc.edu/faculty/projects/Ftrials/scottsboro/scottsb.htm (accessed July 9, 2009); James A. Miller, *Remembering Scottsboro: The Legacy of an Infamous Trial* (Princeton, NJ: Princeton University Press, 2009); PBS, American Experience—"Scottsboro: An American Tragedy" directed by Barak Goodman and Daniel Anker, 90 minutes (2000); Manning Marable and Leith Mullings, eds., *Let Nobody Turn Us Around* (New York: Rowman and Littlefield, 2009), 279–81; Parks, *My Story*, 60–63.

27. Douglas O. Linder, *The Trial of "The Scottsboro Boys," Famous American Trials*, http://www.law.umkc.edu/faculty/projects/Ftrials/scottsboro/scottsb.htm (accessed July 9, 2009).

28. Ibid.

29. Ibid.

30. Ibid.

31. Brinkley, *Rosa Parks*, 40.

32. Parks, *My Story*, 66–67.

33. Parks, *My Story*, 64.

34. James D. Anderson, *The Education of Blacks in the South, 1860–1935* (Chapel Hill: University of North Carolina Press, 1988), 235.

35. Ibid., 236.

36. Parks, *My Story*, 65.

37. "A Half-Century of Learning: Historical Statistics on Educational Attainment in the United States, 1940 to 2000," http://www.census.gov/

population/www/socdemo/education/phct41.html (accessed July 13, 2009).

38. Parks, *My Story*, 65.

39. Brinkley, *Rosa Parks*, 43.

40. Linda Reed, *Simple Decency and Common Sense: The Southern Conference Movement, 1938–1963* (Bloomington, IN: University of Indiana Press, 1991); Thomas A. Krueger, *And Promises to Keep: The Southern Conference for Human Welfare, 1938–1948* (Nashville, TN: Vanderbilt University Press, 1967); Diane McWhorter, *Carry Me Home: Birmingham, Alabama, The Climactic Battle of the Civil Rights Revolution* (New York: Simon and Schuster, 2001); Virginia Foster Durr, *Outside the Magic Circle: The Autobiography of Virginia Foster Durr* (Reprint, Tuscaloosa, AL: University of Alabama Press, 1990); Encyclopedia of Alabama, http://www.encyclopediaofalabama.org/face/Article.jsp?id=h-1593 (accessed August 8, 2009).

41. Encyclopedia of Alabama, http://www.encyclopediaofalabama.org/face/Article.jsp?id=h-1593 (accessed August 8, 2009).

42. Reed, *Simple Decency and Common Sense*; Krueger, *And Promises to Keep*; Encyclopedia of Alabama.

Chapter 3

SEEKING EQUALITY

African Americans had long understood the importance of education in the quest for racial equality. Second only in importance to education was the right to vote. Since Reconstruction, African Americans had fought and died to gain and maintain their right to choose those who would represent them in government. Lawmakers passed legislation and the American people ratified constitutional amendments to secure that right. Officially, the Reconstruction Act of 1867 ensured African Americans the right to vote. The Fourteenth Amendment, ratified in 1868, granted citizenship to all persons born or naturalized in the United States as well as equal protection under the law. The Fifteenth Amendment, ratified in 1870, ensured that American citizens could not be denied the right to vote because of race, color, or previous condition of servitude. Yet despite these efforts, those who endorsed segregation and white supremacy found ways to disenfranchise blacks. White supremacists, especially members of the Ku Klux Klan and other organized vigilante groups, openly used deception, intimidation, violence, and murder to make sure that blacks did not vote. White-controlled state governments implicitly supported these efforts. Rosa Parks was well aware that segregationists did everything they could to prevent blacks from registering to vote.[1]

By 1877 Reconstruction had ended and white supremacists went about eliminating any gains African Americans had made. While intimidation and violence were common tactics in curtailing black voting, other more "respectable" methods were popular as well. Polling places were frequently set up far from black communities, and determined black voters found roads blocked, bridges closed, and ferries out of service on Election Day. At other times, election officials simply changed the polling place without notifying black voters, or sometimes black voters would receive notification of a change but, at the last minute, officials would decide not to change the polling place after all. If white supremacists could not control the vote by any of these methods, then stuffing the ballot boxes would always work. One enthusiastic white voter recounted that sometimes blacks might outvote them, "but we can outcount them."[2] Eventually, white-controlled legislatures helped disenfranchise blacks. Beginning in the 1880s, these state legislators instituted poll taxes, complicated balloting processes, literacy and residency requirements, white primaries, and grandfather clauses to make it nearly impossible for blacks to register and vote. African Americans challenged these methods, especially the poll tax, but even the U.S. Supreme Court upheld the tax as constitutional. Rosa Parks observed that most blacks in Alabama were effectively disenfranchised by the poll tax, since most did not have the money to pay it.[3]

There was one way that some blacks could register to vote. In her autobiography, Rosa explains it: blacks could register if whites would vouch for them, and some blacks resorted to this means to register. Yet they had no interest in helping other blacks to gain the same privilege.[4] This particularly troubled Rosa, especially since this group would tell working-class blacks that they should not be concerned about voting; registered black voters were in favor with the whites and did not want to lose their privileged position. This classic "divide and conquer" system divided blacks against themselves, thus for a time making united action nearly impossible. In the 1940s, some of Montgomery's blacks formed a Voter's League, and Rosa Parks kept the list of registered voters in Montgomery for the league. Rosa remembered that 31 names appeared on the list, and although some of the people on the list had died, their names had not been removed.[5] Obviously, very few African Americans in Montgomery could vote in 1940. Raymond Parks tried to register but was never successful in Alabama. He had white acquaintances who volunteered to vouch for him, but he refused to play that game. According to Rosa, Raymond wanted no one's help to register.[6]

Raymond's thwarted efforts added to Rosa's growing aversion to segregation and second-class citizenship. Her brother Sylvester's experiences in World War II would only add to her revulsion. As the United States prepared to enter World War II, African Americans wondered where they would stand in the wartime society. The Selective Service Act of 1940 contained a clause forbidding discrimination in the drafting and training of men. Despite this clause, for a time draft boards accepted only white men for training, justifying their actions on the grounds that training camps lacked housing facilities for blacks. African Americans protested loudly, but with few positive results. By the fall of 1940, the U.S. Army began to induct

Three African American cadets prepare for a training mission with their white instructor at Tuskegee, Alabama, in September 1942. Their 99th Pursuit Squadron, later known as the Tuskegee Airmen, was the first black combat unit in the U.S. Army Air Corps. (AP Photo)

African Americans on the general basis of their proportion of the African American population of the country. This meant that if African
Americans made up 10 percent of the population in 1940, then
10 percent of the army inductees should be African American. However, except for black medical officers and chaplains, the army organized black soldiers into separate units led by white officers. Most
white officers assigned black soldiers to menial jobs, such as maintenance and supply, and the military services promoted very few blacks.
In 1941, after continuous pressure from the NAACP, the War Department formed the all-black 99th Pursuit Squadron of the U.S. Army
Air Corps to train a small group of pilots, who became better known
as the Tuskegee Airmen because they trained at Tuskegee, Alabama.
The group flew important supply and service missions in North Africa and Europe beginning in 1943. Because of increasing military
demands in 1944, they began flying with white pilots in the European
war, successfully running bombing missions and becoming the only
U.S. unit to sink a German destroyer.[7] Although

> black soldiers were generally restricted from combat, the realities
> of war would soon blur the lines of race....One major break-
> through came during the Battle of the Bulge, in late 1944.
> General Dwight D. Eisenhower, faced with Hitler's advancing
> army on the Western Front, temporarily desegregated the army,
> calling for urgent assistance on the front lines. More than 2,000
> black soldiers volunteered to fight.[8]

Rosa's brother Sylvester, drafted in the early 1940s, served in both
Europe and the Pacific.[9] The Army assigned Sylvester to the 1318th
Medical Detachment's Engineering Services Regiment, where he
served as a medic during the Battle of Normandy and later in the South
Seas. A private first class, Sylvester carried wounded soldiers from the
battlefields, caring for them in improvised ambulances and in military
hospitals.[10] He was one of many blacks who served with distinction.
Many units received the Presidential Distinguished Unit Citation for
their bravery; individuals received recognition that ranged from good
conduct medals to the Distinguished Service Cross; and 82 black pilots
received the Distinguished Flying Cross.[11]

Like many African Americans at the time, Rosa Parks believed that by fighting to defend American democracy, blacks would gain the rights America had long denied them. To ensure that this would be the outcome, African Americans mounted what they called the "Double V" campaign—victory abroad, victory at home. Retired U.S. Army Colonel Bill De Shields, a historian and founder of The Black Military History Institute of America in Annapolis, Maryland, says,

> The symbol of black participation at that time was "the Double V" in other words, "Double V" meant two victories: victory against the enemy abroad, and victory against the enemy at home. The enemy at home of course being racism, discrimination, prejudice and Jim Crow.[12]

Segregationists had other ideas. After the American military achieved victory abroad, the South once again thrust returning black soldiers into the legalized system of segregation. Many tried to register to vote and failed; most were treated with even less respect than before they fought. White segregationists believed that things should return to the way they had been before the war, but black veterans resisted. Some retaliated, some lost their lives. Sylvester and many others simply left the South. No longer willing to tolerate demeaning treatment in postwar Montgomery, unable to find a job, and resolved to provide for himself and his family, Sylvester moved with his family north to Detroit.[13] The particularly outrageous injustices endured by black veterans were another catalyst for Rosa Parks's decision to engage in public activism. In December 1943, she joined the Montgomery chapter of the NAACP.

African Americans in Alabama were among the first black southerners to establish an NAACP chapter. In 1913, faculty, staff, and local citizens connected with Talladega College, in the town of Talladega, organized an NAACP branch four years before any other southern state.

> This first branch lasted only a year, however, because college officials dismissed William Pickens, who had been an organizer for the national NAACP office since 1910. Talladega College officials charged the controversial professor of languages with insubordination, promoting strife between white administrators and black

students, and excessive absences from classes for his time spent recruiting and fundraising for the NAACP's New York office.[14]

The onset of World War I, however, reinvigorated the NAACP in the state. African Americans quickly saw the hypocrisy between the rhetoric of a war to "make the world safe for democracy" and the inequality of Jim Crow segregation in Alabama and other southern states. This was especially true for blacks serving in the military.

The NAACP, with its already strong reputation for fighting segregation, quickly gained a large following in the state. In 1918, the first of 13 post–World War I branches was founded in Montgomery. African Americans in Alabama soon formed NAACP branches across the state in industrial regions, farming areas, and in cities large and small.[15]

In the1940s, the NAACP's membership in Alabama grew substantially. Within a few years, there were 35 branches with nearly 15,000 members. Much of this increase was driven by a number of successful court cases filed by the national office to challenge discrimination in housing, public spaces, and education. However, growing outrage among blacks in Alabama with racial biases heightened by America's entry into World War II served to increase membership as well. Racist policies in the military and wartime industries increased resentment. The result was an explosion in NAACP activism in the state and throughout the South.

These efforts expanded further in 1945, when Alabama NAACP leaders—headed by Birmingham branch president Emory Jackson, Montgomery branch leader Edgar Daniel (E. D.) Nixon and Mobile branch secretary John L. LeFlore—formed a statewide conference of branches that provided opportunities for developing a common approach to eliminating white supremacy and offered occasions for fundraising unavailable to individual branches.[16]

Although most NAACP members were men, women began joining the organization in large numbers in the late 1930s. By the early 1940s, women constituted more than 55 percent of the total membership of the Montgomery branch and made up more than 20 percent of the executive committee.[17] Several women, including Rosa Parks, held the post of secretary of the Montgomery NAACP—an extremely important position, given this officer's role as the principal link with the New York headquarters.

By 1934, Raymond Parks had left the NAACP, disillusioned by what he perceived as its "elitist" leadership. In 1943, however, Rosa Parks decided to join. In later years she recalled that she did not realize that there were any women in the local organization

> until I saw in the *Alabama Tribune* a picture of Johnnie Carr, my friend and classmate at Miss White's school. She was the only female member.... The article said that Johnnie was working with the Montgomery branch... so I thought "Maybe one time I'll go over to the NAACP and see if I can run into Johnnie."[18]

In December 1943, Rosa Parks went to her first NAACP meeting. Johnnie Mae Carr was not at that meeting, but Rosa stayed and paid her membership dues. She was the only woman in attendance at the meeting, and the men said they needed a secretary. She remembered, "I was too timid to say no. I just started taking minutes, and that was the way I was elected secretary."[19] Rosa Parks and Johnnie Mae Carr were the only two women in Montgomery to regularly attend NAACP meetings.[20]

According to historian Douglas Brinkley, Rosa Parks had other reasons for joining the NAACP in 1943. The first was her admiration for Walter White. White was a long-time civil rights advocate. In 1916, he established an NAACP branch in his hometown of Atlanta, Georgia; he was assistant secretary of the NAACP from 1918 until 1931 and executive secretary from 1931 to 1955. Like Rosa's grandfather and husband, Walter White was very light-skinned, and he also he had blue eyes and blond hair. White's primary responsibility in the NAACP was conducting undercover investigations of lynching and race riots. By going under cover and passing as a white man, White was able to question members of

> lynch mobs and other whites who had witnessed or were involved in racial violence. He tricked them into giving him candid

accounts that the NAACP would then publicize. During these years, White investigated forty-one lynchings and eight race riots, including the riots in Elaine, Arkansas, and Chicago, Illinois, during the Red Summer of 1919. On more than one occasion he narrowly escaped vigilantes who discovered his true identity.[21]

Although Walter White could have passed for a white man, he embraced his African American heritage. In the opening lines of his autobiography, *A Man Called White*, he proudly proclaims, "I am a Negro, but my skin is white, my eyes are blue, and my hair is blond. The traits of my race are nowhere visible upon me."[22] Rosa Parks admired this as well as White's ability to push for black rights at the local, state, and national political levels.

Rosa Parks's efforts to register to vote in 1943 influenced her decision to join the NAACP as well. Registering to vote was not an easy task for African Americans in the South in the 1940s. The office of the registrar of voters was open only at very specific times, and those hours were not widely publicized. People wishing to register had to call to ask when the office would be open, and on many occasions the hours were set for midmorning, when most African Americans were at work. As Rosa later recounted, negotiating these hurdles and taking off from work to go to the office did not ensure that blacks would be able to register; the office would close at noon regardless of how many people were waiting or how long they had been in line.[23] Even getting through the door did not guarantee registration.

Until the passage of the Voting Rights Act in 1965, the states, not the federal government, decided the eligibility requirements for voters. When Rosa Parks tried to register to vote in 1943, the Alabama Constitution of 1901 was still in effect. This constitution had many provisions detailing the exact qualifications for voters, most of which were designed to disenfranchise blacks. Article VIII, Section 178, required voters to "have resided in the state at least two years, in the county one year, and in the precinct or ward three months, immediately preceding the election at which he offers to vote," while Section 180 specified that only "persons who are of good character and who understand the duties and obligations of citizenship" could be registered. In addition, Section 181 required Alabama voters to be literate and demonstrate an understanding of the U.S. Constitution, specifying only those "who can read and write any article of the Constitution of the United States in the English language" could be registered to vote. Potential voters had to own a specific amount of taxable property as well.

> The owner in good faith in his own right, or the husband of a woman who is the owner in good faith, in her own right, of forty acres of land situate in this state, upon which they reside; or the owner in good faith in his own right, or the husband of any woman who is the owner in good faith, in her own right, of real estate situate in this state, assessed for taxation at the value of three hundred dollars or more, or the owner in good faith, in his own right, or the husband of a woman who is the owner in good faith, in her own right, of personal property in this state assessed for taxation at three hundred dollars or more; provided, that the taxes due upon such real or personal property for the year next preceding the year in which he offers to register shall have been paid.[24]

If any of these provisions did not disqualify black voters, Section 182 contained a laundry list of other restrictions that registrars could use to disqualify applicants. Section 186 gave registrars the power to "examine, under oath or affirmation, all applicants for registration, and to take testimony touching the qualifications of such applicants," and Section 194 required payment of a poll tax of $1.50 per year.[25]

The first time Rosa went to the registrar's office, she apparently did not qualify because she did not receive her voter certificate, although the registrar offered no explanation. The next time she tried to register, the registrar denied her application as well. When she asked why, she was told that she had not passed. Under the state constitution, registrars did not have to provide any evidence justifying their decisions. Nevertheless, Rosa believed she had passed the test and, in 1945, she tried again. This time, she remembered, she took the precaution of making a copy of her answers to the 21 questions: "I copied them out by hand. I was going to keep that copy and use it to bring suit against the voter-registration board."[26] In fact, she brought E. D. Nixon, head of the Montgomery NAACP, and Arthur A. Madison, a black attorney, to the registrar's office with her. Perhaps the registrar saw Rosa making a copy of her answers, perhaps he saw Nixon and Madison and surmised that Rosa was contemplating a lawsuit, or perhaps not—but this time she received her voter registration card in the mail.

Rosa Parks was now a registered voter, but she still had to pay her poll tax of $1.50 retroactively to the age of 21. By the time Rosa was able to register, she was 32 years old, which meant that she would have to pay the $1.50 for each of 11 years, even though the state had denied her the right to vote for those 11 years. Nevertheless, Rosa put together the $16.50 required, a considerable amount of money in 1945, and paid the tax.[27] In the next gubernatorial election, she voted for Jim Folsom, who was running against Handy Ellis, an openly racist candidate. Rosa experienced no difficulties voting, later noting that after all of her determined efforts, voting had proved to be "simple and uneventful."[28]

Ironically, it was during her second attempt at voter registration that Rosa Parks first encountered a bigoted bus driver by the name of James F. Blake. African American passengers on the city buses were subject to special rules, many of which were arbitrarily enforced, depending on the driver. Black passengers were required to step through the front door to pay their fare, then get off and go to the back door to board. Some drivers found it amusing to pull away before the black passenger could reach the back door. Another rule applied to seating. Each city bus had 36 seats. The first 10 were reserved for whites even if no white passengers were on the bus. The 10 seats in the back were theoretically for black passengers, and a movable barrier designated the colored section. Drivers used the 16 seats in the middle for white or black passengers at their discretion. If the first 10 seats filled with white passengers and additional white passengers would have to stand, the driver would move the barrier and require any black passengers to move to the back of the bus. If black passengers filled the last 10 seats, additional black passengers would have to stand even if the white section was empty. Drivers had absolute power over the seating of the passengers; many carried guns and had police power to enforce segregation rules on the buses.[29]

On this particular day the back of the bus, even including the back stairwell, was full of black passengers. Rosa Parks entered the bus in the front, paid her fare, and walked up the aisle through the white section to stand in the back. When she turned around, she saw Blake, the driver, glaring at her. He told her to get off the bus and go to the back door to get on. She refused. She was already in the back and saw no need to get off and get back on. Blake then screamed at her, saying that if she did not get off and get back on through the back door she would need to get off "his bus," When she refused to move, Blake grabbed her coat sleeve and pushed her forward. Near the front of the bus, Rosa dropped her purse. She remembered, "Rather than stoop or bend over to get it, I sat right down in the front seat and from a sitting position I picked up my purse." According to Rosa, Blake looked like he wanted to hit her, but did not strike her. She did not get back on the bus through the rear door, and from that point on, she habitually checked who was driving the bus before boarding.[30] Rosa Parks would encounter James Blake again.

Finally, Rosa Parks was comfortable in joining the NAACP because of its leadership. Edgar Daniel (better known as E. D.) Nixon was president of the local NAACP chapter and one of the most active African Americans in Montgomery. Born on July 12, 1899, in Lowndes County, Alabama, Nixon lived most of his life in Montgomery. Although he had little formal education, he was a naturally charismatic leader. He was six feet, four inches tall, possessed a deep baritone voice, and had a natural ability to organize and rally people around a cause.

In the early 1920s, Nixon began working as a Pullman sleeping car porter. Porters assisted passengers boarding trains and carried their luggage. Sleeping car porters assisted those passengers who took residence in the sleeping compartments of the trains. Widely considered desirable among African Americans for the high wages and travel opportunities they offered, Pullman porter jobs allowed these men to enter the small middle class of black America. During his travels on the trains, Nixon was exposed to the less restrictive communities and social practices outside the Deep South, with its entrenched Jim Crow racial policies. It also introduced him to the BSCP, a union that advocated better wages and working conditions for black railway workers, and acquainted him with its influential leader, A. Phillip Randolph. It was through these connections and experiences that Nixon was inspired to become an activist.[31]

During the 1940s, Nixon and a group of African Americans formed the Alabama Voters League, working with attorney Arthur A. Madison to increase black voter registration in Montgomery. Sometimes called the "father of the civil rights movement," Nixon "organized and launched a march of about 750 people on the Montgomery County Municipal Court House in 1944 to raise awareness of impediments to black voting."[32] Rosa Parks met Nixon through the Alabama Voters League. In 1945, Nixon served as president of the Montgomery branch of the NAACP and two years later became state president of the organization. Rosa Parks remembered Nixon as "a proud dignified man who carried himself straight as an arrow."[33]

As secretary of the Montgomery NAACP, Rosa Parks spent a great deal of time at Nixon's office, keeping the office running while Nixon was on long railroad runs in his job as a Pullman porter. She tracked and forwarded membership payments to the national office in New York, fielded phone calls, conducted correspondence, and distributed press releases.[34] With Nixon, Rosa worked on cases involving rape, murder, and discrimination. Unfortunately, someone cleaning out the office later inadvertently threw away the boxes of her notes. Nevertheless, several of the cases stood out in her mind, and she related the events of those cases in her autobiography. One case involved one of the paroled Scottsboro Boys, Andy Wright. Wright violated his parole by leaving the state to visit his mother in Tennessee. The police rearrested him for this parole violation in August 1946. During his subsequent incarceration, Rosa Parks, Zenobia Johnson, W. G. Porter, J. E. Pierce, and E. D. Nixon formed his defense committee. They met with the parole board in support of Wright and successfully convinced the board to release him. The Montgomery NAACP then found Wright a job driving a truck and kept in touch with him.[35]

Another case involved the rape of a black woman, Recy Taylor, of Abbeville, Alabama, by six white men. The men kidnapped Taylor as she was walking home from church and forced her into a car at gun- and knifepoint in September 1944. Then they raped her. Although the sheriff arrested all of the men, the county grand jury refused to indict them even though the driver confessed and named the other five men involved. Both black and white citizens were horror-struck by the gross injustice and formed the Committee for Equal Justice, led by Caroline Bellin, a white woman. Bellin asked the Montgomery NAACP to help with the case. The NAACP was successful in getting Governor Chauncey Sparks to convene a special grand jury, but they too refused to indict the men.[36] This was not how things worked out when a white woman accused a black man of rape.

In 1952, Jeremiah Reeves, an 18-year-old delivery driver, was having a relationship with a white woman on his delivery route. When the woman's neighbors began to notice the frequency of his deliveries, one of the neighbor's looked in a window and saw the couple undressing. As was common at the time, when the woman noticed someone looking in, she screamed that Jeremiah was raping her. The police quickly arrested Jeremiah and a jury sentenced him to death despite the fact that there was no evidence of rape other than the woman's word. In 1954, the U.S. Supreme Court overturned Reeves's conviction, but after only two days of testimony and 34 minutes of deliberation, a second Alabama jury found Reeves guilty again. They again sentenced him to death.[37] The Montgomery NAACP worked for several years to save Jeremiah Reeves, but ultimately they failed. On March 28, 1958, after spending six years on death row, Jeremiah was electrocuted by the state of Alabama at Montgomery's Kilby State Prison.[38]

Nine days later, on Easter Sunday, a young minister named Martin Luther King, Jr., addressed two thousand people at the Alabama State Capitol.

> The issue before us now is not the innocence or guilt of Jeremiah Reeves. Even if he were guilty, it is the severity and the inequality of the penalty that constitutes the injustice. Full grown white men committing comparable crimes against Negro girls are rarely if ever punished, and never given the death penalty or even a life sentence.... Easter is a day of hope.... It is a day that says to us that the forces of evil and injustice cannot survive.... We must live and face death if necessary with that hope.[39]

Reeves's ordeal had a chilling effect on many African Americans, young and old. His arrest, speedy trial, quick conviction, and subsequent execution radicalized many African Americans in Montgomery, with consequences that would become apparent in the coming years.

NOTES

1. Rosa Parks, *My Story* (New York: Penguin Books, 1992), 71.

2. John Hope Franklin and Alfred A. Moss, *From Slavery to Freedom*, 8th ed. (New York: McGraw Hill, 2000), 282.

3. Douglas Brinkley, *Rosa Parks; A Life* (New York: Penguin Books, 2000), 47.

4. Parks, *My Story*, 71.

5. Ibid., 72.

6. Ibid.

7. Lisa Krause, "Black Soldiers in WW II: Fighting Enemies at Home and Abroad," *National Geographic News* (February 15, 2001), http://news.nationalgeographic.com/news/2001/02/0215_tuskegee.html (accessed July 15, 2009).

8. Ibid.

9. Parks, *My Story*, 90.

10. Brinkley, *Rosa Parks*, 62.

11. Franklin and Moss, *From Slavery to Freedom*, 491.

12. "African-American Soldiers in World War II Helped Pave Way for Integration of US Military," http://www.voanews.com/english/archive/2005–05/2005–05–10-voa47.cfm (accessed July 15, 2009).

13. Parks, *My Story*, 92–93.

14. "National Association for the Advancement of Colored People in Alabama," http://www.encyclopediaofalabama.org/face/Article.jsp?id=h-1670 (accessed July 15, 2009).

15. Ibid.

16. Ibid.

17. Ibid.

18. Parks, *My Story*, 80–81.

19. Ibid., 81; Marcia M. Greenlee, "Interview with Rosa McCauley Parks" on August 22 and 23, 1978, in *The Black Woman Oral History Project*, vol. 8, ed. Ruth Edmonds Hill (Westport, CT: Meckler, 1991), 253.

20. Parks, *My Story*, 81.

21. Walter White (1893–1955), http://www.georgiaencyclopedia.org/nge/Article.jsp?id=h-747 (accessed July 16, 2009).

22. Walter White, *A Man Called White: The Autobiography of Walter White* (New York: Viking Press, 1948), 3.

23. Parks, *My Story*, 74.

24. Constitution of Alabama, http://www.legislature.state.al.us/CodeOfAlabama/Constitution/1901/Constitution1901_toc.htm (accessed July 16, 2009).

25. Ibid.

26. Parks, My Story, 75.

27. Ibid., 75–76.

28. Ibid., 76.

29. JoAnn Robinson, The Montgomery Bus Boycott and the Women Who Started It (Knoxville: University of Tennessee Press, 1987), 34–36; Parks, My Story, 76–77.

30. Parks, My Story, 78–79.

31. E. D. Nixon Collection, Special Collections, Levi Watkins Library, Alabama State University, Montgomery; E. D. Nixon, http://www.encyclopediaofalabama.org/face/Article.jsp?id=h-1355 (accessed July 17, 2009).

32. Ibid.

33. Parks, My Story, 73.

34. Ibid., 84.

35. Ibid., 83–84.

36. Ibid., 84–85.

37. Phillip Hoose, Claudette Colvin: Twice Toward Justice (Los Angeles: Farrar, Straus and Giroux, 2000), 23–24.

38. Ibid., 115; Parks, My Story, 85–86.

39. Clayborne Carson, ed., The Papers of Martin Luther King, Jr., vol. IV, Symbol of the Movement, January 1957–December 1958, "Statement Delivered at the Prayer Pilgrimage Protesting the Electrocution of Jeremiah Reeves" (Berkeley: University of California Press, 2007), 396–97.

Chapter 4

GROWING ACTIVISM

By the time Rosa Parks joined the NAACP in 1943, the organization had already had a 34-year history of fighting racial violence, discrimination, and segregation. In 1917, NAACP attorneys won the Supreme Court case of *Buchanan v. Warley*, which ruled that states could not restrict and officially segregate African Americans into residential districts. It had fought and won the battle for the commission of African American officers in World War I. It had fought against lynching calling for an antilynching bill and widely publicizing violence against African Americans. By 1935, NAACP lawyers Charles Houston and Thurgood Marshall won the legal battle to admit a black student to the University of Maryland. In addition, during World War II, the NAACP took part in the effort to ensure that President Franklin Roosevelt supported a nondiscrimination policy in war-related industries and federal employment, and it supported the "Double V" campaign.[1]

In postwar America, many of the issues blacks faced remained the same, but African American reactions to them changed. According to historian Douglas Brinkley, 500,000 black soldiers fought in Europe and the Pacific during World War II, while another 500,000 blacks served on the home front. By 1944, a total of 701,678 blacks had served in the U.S. Army; about 165,000 were in the Navy; 5,000 joined the Coast Guard; and 17,000 served as Marines.[2] At war's end, black organizations—including new political, civic, labor, and religious groups, and especially the NAACP—began to push much harder for black equality. Nevertheless, black servicemen returning to the South faced the humiliation of Jim Crow segregation and intensified violence by the Ku Klux Klan (KKK) while Dixiecrat politicians called for renewed vigilance in enforcing "separate but equal." In fact, decorated black soldiers returning from war seemed to fuel antiblack sentiment. In 1946, Sergeant Isaac Woodard, on furlough from his duties in the South Pacific, boarded a bus in Georgia. The driver believed he was acting "uppity" when he took too long in the "Colored Only" rest room at a stop in South Carolina. The bus driver called the sheriff in the next town to report a drunken ex-soldier on his bus. When the bus pulled into Aiken, South Carolina, the police pulled Woodard off the bus and beat him with blackjacks and nightsticks. A court convicted Woodard of public intoxication; he was fined $50 and then thrown into a cell. Eventually the police transferred him to a military hospital in Spartanburg to treat his shattered ribs and severely damaged eyes. Woodard lost his sight because of this ruthless attack. According to Rosa Parks, an all-white jury took just 15 minutes to acquit the police officer accused of blinding him.[3] It did not matter that Woodard was a decorated soldier and did not drink; his allegedly "uppity" behavior and his uniform were all that the judge needed to establish his guilt. African Americans now called on President Harry S. Truman to act. Black banker, educator, and Spanish-American war veteran R. R. Wright wrote to the president,

> Now, Mr. President, I think it is a terrible disgrace to our beloved South and to the United States, that a returned veteran who has risked his life for the purpose of maintaining freedom of our country, is not permitted to travel in his own native country, subject to decent treatment by the officers of the land, without being beaten unmercifully and deprived of his eyes.[4]

By 1946, tempers were running high throughout the South. In Georgia, four white men shot Macio Snipes in his front yard because he dared to vote.[5] Then, on July 25, 1946, some 50 miles east of Atlanta, Georgia, an angry mob of white men ambushed two young African American couples at the Moore's Ford Bridge. The men pulled all four—George Dorsey, 28, his wife Mae Murray Dorsey, 23, his sister, Dorothy Dorsey Malcom, 20, and Roger Malcom, 24—from a car, beat them, and shot them to death. There were many theories about the cause of the crime; many people believed that local residents might have considered George Dorsey "uppity" since returning from service in World War II. Whites accused George of carousing with white women as well. The lynching took place in broad daylight by unmasked gunmen, but according to Bobby Howard, a civil rights activist who has been investigating the crime since 1968, "the tight-knit people of Walton County created a perfect cover-up." According to Howard, after the lynching, "white people formed a code of silence, and black people, expecting violent repercussions if they spoke up, were scared into silence. Even local law enforcement officers were tight-lipped."[6] At the time of the lynching, President Truman sent the FBI to investigate the crime, known as the Moore's Ford lynching, because George Dorsey, who had served in World War II, had been home for only 10 months before he was murdered by the mob. Although the FBI recovered bullets from shotguns and pistols of various calibers, and despite large demonstrations at the time in New York and Washington, D.C., as of 2006 the crime remained unsolved.[7]

Rosa's brother Sylvester endured a multitude of indignities as well when he returned to Alabama in 1945. According to Douglas Brinkley, some whites spat on him, the local police declared him "uppity," and he found it impossible to find work in Montgomery. Rather than being honored for his service in saving lives, white racists maligned Sylvester and treated him as a troublemaker. Rosa recalled that many black World War II veterans, particularly when they were in uniform, actually encountered more disrespect than they had before the war.[8] Her brother and his family did not stay in Alabama; they packed their things and moved to Detroit, where Sylvester found a job as a janitor in a Chrysler factory. According to Rosa, Sylvester never returned to Alabama, not even to visit his mother and sister.[9]

These incidents and hundreds more prompted President Truman to take several actions on civil rights. On September 19, 1946, Truman

met with a delegation from the National Emergency Committee against
Mob Violence proposing to appoint an investigatory committee deal-
ing with civil rights. Four days later, he met with representatives of the
National Conference on Lynching led by Paul Robeson.[10] Although
these may seem like token gestures, Truman was ahead of public opinion on the matter of civil rights. His commitment to the advancement
of black civil rights would continue to strengthen. In June 1947, Truman was the first American president to address the NAACP. On the
steps of the Lincoln Memorial to a crowd of ten thousand people, President Truman called for the guarantee of full civil rights and freedom
for *all* Americans. With Walter White, head of the NAACP, standing
beside him, Truman said:

> When I say all Americans, I mean all Americans.
> Many of our people still suffer the indignity of insult, the nar-
> rowing fear of intimidation, and, I regret to say, the threat of phys-
> ical and mob violence. Prejudice and intolerance in which these
> evils are rooted still exist. The conscience of our nation, the legal
> machinery which enforces it, have not yet secured to each citizen
> full freedom of fear.
> We cannot wait another decade or another generation to
> remedy these evils. We must work, as never before, to cure them
> now.[11]

Truman then went on to call for state and federal action against lynching and the poll tax and an end to inequality and the American caste
system based on race or color. Walter White called his speech "coura-
geous" in its "condemnations of evils based upon race prejudice...and
its call for immediate action against them."[12]

Later in 1946, Truman put his future on the line when he established
a blue-ribbon commission on civil rights chaired by Charles Wilson,
head of General Electric. Walter White and other black leaders clearly
recognized that Truman's actions were "nothing short of political sui-
cide," yet the president did not back down. After the speech he turned
to Walter White and said he meant "every word of it—and I'm going to
prove that I do mean it." In October 1946, Truman's civil rights commission issued its report, titled *To Secure These Rights*. In February 1948,

*Accompanied by former First Lady Eleanor Roosevelt and Walter White, execu-
tive secretary of the NAACP, President Harry S. Truman (left) strides toward
the steps of the Lincoln Memorial to address the NAACP on June 29, 1947.
(AP Photo/Harvey Georges)*

Truman used the finding of the report to send an unprecedented civil
rights message to Congress, in which he said:

> Not all groups are free to live and work where they please of to im-
> prove their conditions of life by their own efforts. Not all groups
> enjoy the full privileges of citizenship....
>
> The Federal Government has a clear duty to see that the Con-
> stitutional guarantees of individual liberties and equal protection
> under the laws are not denied or abridged anywhere in the Union.
> That duty is shared by all three branches of the Government, but
> it can be filled only is the Congress enacts modern civil rights
> laws, adequate to the needs of the day, and demonstrating our
> continuing faith in the free way of life.[13]

The president then called for an antilynching law, more effective
statutes to protect voting rights, the abolition of the poll tax, a permanent Fair Employment Practices Commission to end discrimination
in employment and union membership, and the end to segregation
in interstate travel and in the federal government. Finally, Truman

announced that he was examining ways to end discrimination in the armed forces. And on July 26, 1948, Executive Order 9981 declared that "there shall be equality of treatment and opportunity for all persons in the armed services without regard to race, color, religion or national origin." Five days later, the *Chicago Defender*, one of the most powerful black-owned and black-edited newspapers in the country, published the headline "President Truman Wipes Out Segregation In Armed Forces." This was the first time a president had used an executive order to implement civil rights.[14] Harry Truman became president in 1945 after the death of President Franklin Roosevelt. In 1948, the American people elected Truman to his first full term as president. At Truman's inauguration in January 1949, for the first time in the history of Washington, D.C., black guests stayed at several of the best hotels, since Truman had ordered that "black Americans were to be as welcome as anyone at the main events of the inaugural."[15]

These actions are all the more significant when we take Truman's personal background into consideration. His ancestors were Confederates and he came from a part of Missouri where Jim Crow was still practiced in 1948. When he was approached by southern Democrats who suggested he "soften" his views on race relations, Truman said,

> But my very stomach turned over when I learned that Negro soldiers just back from overseas, were being dumped out of army trucks in Mississippi and beaten. Whatever my inclinations as a native of Missouri might have been, as President I know this is bad. I shall fight to end evil like this.[16]

On a personal level, Truman continued to retain some of his biases and old habits of speech, but as president, he knew he could not sit by and do nothing in the face of glaring injustice. The murder of black soldiers was repugnant. As chapter secretary of the Montgomery NAACP, Rosa Parks certainly would have been aware of these changes taking place in Washington. She would know as well that NAACP membership was on the rise. By 1943, membership had reached 250,000 and by 1944, some 429,000 Americans had joined the association.[17]

After Sylvester moved his family to Detroit, Rosa traveled to the city for a two-week visit. She was astounded by the big city and the fact that she could sit anywhere on a city bus and get good accommodations. Sylvester took his sister on an auto tour of the area and they visited the Detroit Art Institute. The Second Baptist Church impressed her. Sylvester wanted Rosa, Raymond, and his mother Leona to leave Montgomery and move to Detroit. Rosa was hesitant. Despite the north's reputation as the "Promised Land" for black Americans, racial discrimination and violence were common there as well. In 1943, for example, a riot broke out in Detroit between blacks and whites. The situation had been tense for months. High levels of wartime migration led to intense competition over housing, transportation, recreation, and education.

> Blacks who believed they were heading to a promised land found a northern bigotry every bit as pervasive and virulent as what they thought they had left behind in the Deep South. And southern whites brought their own traditional prejudices with them as both races migrated northward.[18]

Tensions continued to rise along with the growing black population. By 1943, the number of blacks in Detroit had doubled since 1933 to 200,000. Then, on June 20,

> blacks and whites clashed in minor skirmishes on Belle Isle. Two young blacks, angered that they had been ejected from Eastwood Park some five days previously, had gone to Belle Isle to try to even the score. Police began to search cars of blacks crossing to Belle Isle but they did not search cars driven by whites. Fighting on the island began around 10 P.M. and police declared it under control by midnight. More than 200 blacks and whites had participated in the free-for-all.[19]

The police did not have it under control. Leo Tipton and Charles Lyons told a black crowd at the Forest Social Club that whites had thrown a black woman and her baby off the Belle Isle Bridge. An angry crowd of more than 500 poured onto the street, breaking windows and looting stores. Meanwhile, rumors spread within the white community as well: blacks had raped and murdered a white woman on the Belle

Isle Bridge. An angry mob of whites took to the streets, beating blacks as they were getting off streetcars. A melee ensued. The police could not control it, so the mayor called on President Franklin D. Roosevelt for help. Federal troops moved into the area and things began to calm down. In the end, 34 people died, 25 of them black. Police and federal troops arrested more than 1,800 for looting and other incidents, the vast majority black. Thirteen murders remained unsolved. At trial, juries sentenced five black men to 80-day jail terms for disturbing the peace, while acquitting two. Police charged 28, who were later, convicted, of various charges including carrying concealed weapons, destruction of property, assault, and larceny. The court sentenced Tipton and Little, the two blacks linked to the original rumor, to two to five years for inciting a riot.[20]

According to historian Douglas Brinkley, Rosa realized that Detroit was not an oasis of racial tolerance. In a radio interview explaining her decision to remain in Montgomery, she later said, "Racism was almost as widespread in Detroit as in Montgomery. And my husband, Raymond, wanted to stay in Alabama. So we put aside any ideas of moving to a northern promised land that wasn't."[21] Other areas experienced race riots as well: Newark, Harlem, Los Angeles, and Little Rock. Rosa was well aware that there was no promised land for African Americans in the 1940s.

Therefore Rosa, Raymond, and Leona remained in Montgomery. Rosa took a job altering clothing at Crittenden's Tailor Shop and later at the Montgomery Fair Department Store. She attended NAACP meetings, working behind the scenes keeping records, registering membership payments, and keeping up with E. D. Nixon's correspondence. She read journals and black newspapers, issuing regular news releases to local and regional newspapers about topics that were important to African Americans. Rosa balanced the books and kept track of reported incidents of racial discrimination. Occasionally she did field research, traveling to interview blacks about legal complaints and recording statements of those who had witnessed lynchings in rural areas.[22] Unfortunately, as Douglas Brinkley has written, in the 1960s, a friend of E. D. Nixon's inadvertently threw away the NAACP files Rosa Parks had kept. According to Rosa, much was lost, because she and Nixon had followed and documented many cases, yet justice had proved elusive.

The effort came to be more of an attempt to confront a discriminatory system and serve notice that African Americans were not content to be second-class citizens.[23]

In 1946, Rosa Parks met Ella Baker, another African American woman who not only affect her activism but would later become a key player in the 1955 bus boycott as well. Born on December 13, 1903, in Norfolk, Virginia, Ella Baker grew up in North Carolina and developed a sense of social justice early in her life. Anna Baker, Ella's mother, served as her role model. Anna fed the hungry and served as a midwife to the women in the community. According to Baker, Anna "was a force," enforcing strict standards of speech, decorum, religiosity, and neighborliness in the family. Anna made sure that Ella received an education and taught her to read before she went to school. After receiving a high school diploma, Baker studied at Shaw University in Raleigh, North Carolina, where she challenged school policies that she thought were unfair. After graduating in 1927 as class valedictorian, she moved to New York City and began joining social activist organizations. In 1930, she joined the Young Negroes Cooperative League, whose purpose was to develop black economic power through collective planning. She also involved herself with several women's organizations. Ella Baker began her involvement with the NAACP in 1940. She worked as a field secretary and then served as director of branches from 1943 until 1946.[24] Baker designed leadership conferences to help branch leaders focus their actions. Between 1944 and 1946, Baker held 10 conferences that covered topics such as how to develop techniques and strategies for group action; she also examined the postwar problems of individual branches. According to Baker, the purpose of the conferences was to "emphasize basic technique and procedure for developing and carrying out local programs of action."[25] However, Baker strongly believed in "participatory democracy" and the development of local leadership. Through these conferences, she hoped that local leaders would take action to influence the national program and policy of the NAACP. Ella Baker met Rosa Parks when she attended an NAACP leadership training conference in Jacksonville, Florida.[26]

By 1949, Rosa Parks was both secretary of the Montgomery NAACP and adviser to the local NAACP Youth Council. Although Rosa never had children of her own, she enjoyed working with young people. E. D. Nixon recalled, "Kids just love Mrs. Parks to death. They had a special bond, an understanding, that was very rare indeed, full of hugs and all that."[27] Perhaps the relationship between Rosa and the young people worked so well because she listened to them and developed projects that served their interests. Rosa recalled that one important project for the youth group was to desegregate the public library. The library open to blacks (the "colored library") was located across town; it was underfunded and had limited holdings. If a student needed a book that was not available at the colored branch, he or she would have to request the book from the main library and wait for the main branch to send it to the colored branch, where it could then be picked up. Both Rosa and E. D. Nixon coached the children as they mounted a campaign to desegregate the main public library. Unfortunately they did not succeed, despite repeated attempts.[28]

In May 1949, Rosa resigned as secretary of the Montgomery NAACP to care for her ailing mother. Nevertheless, she remained involved and inspired through her church—St. Paul AME. She taught Sunday school and heard civil rights sermons from the pulpit. After E. D. Nixon lost his reelection bid for the presidency of the Montgomery NAACP chapter in 1950, Rosa became a "freelance" assistant to him in his Brotherhood of Sleeping Car Porters office. She answered his mail, filed his paperwork, and returned phone calls when he was traveling the country because of his work. In 1952, Rosa returned to the local NAACP office, once again serving as branch secretary. It was there, in June 1953, that Rosa Parks became familiar with the concept of a citywide bus boycott. This boycott was one element in setting the stage for the Montgomery boycott two years later.[29]

This earlier boycott took place in Baton Rouge, Louisiana. In January 1953, the Baton Rouge City Council voted to raise bus fares from 10 to 15 cents. The increase angered African American passengers, who made up about 80 percent of the riders, especially because although they paid full fare, they were required to sit of stand in the back of the bus even if the first ten rows of seats, reserved for white passengers, remained empty. In early February, Reverend T. J. Jemison, the pastor of Mt. Zion Baptist Church, denounced the increase and asked that reserved seating be abolished. At a subsequent meeting at the end of February, the council voted to end reserved seating but required that blacks board the bus from back to front, and no African American passenger was to sit next to or in front of a white passenger. The number of black or white passengers aboard any bus would determine where the line of segregation began. The council then passed Ordinance 222, the new seating law, unanimously. It was to take effect on March 19, 1953.[30]

Three months passed and the bus drivers were still not enforcing Ordinance 222. The first 10 seats on the city buses remained reserved for whites even on routes that primarily served black neighborhoods. In June,

> African Americans demanded enforcement of the law after a bus driver manhandled a black woman who tried to sit in one of the "reserved" seats. Because of this incident, bus company officials ordered their drivers to comply with Ordinance 222. Elated by the enforcement decision, black leaders printed a flier that outlined the provisions of the ordinance and advised black passengers not to give up their seats if ordered to by the drivers.[31]

When Reverend Jemison decided to test the bus company's new rules, the driver ordered him to move and he refused. "The driver drove the bus directly to the police station, and an officer boarded the bus. The officer sided with the black minister over the white driver. Other incidents followed." The bus company suspended two drivers for not complying with Ordinance 222. Angry over challenges to their authority, the drivers went on strike to protest the ordinance. Louisiana's attorney declared the law unconstitutional because it violated existing segregation legislation. Content with the ruling, their power restored, the drivers returned to work.[32]

African American passengers, however, were not content with the ruling. Under the leadership of Reverend Jemison and Raymond Scott, a tailor, blacks formed the United Defense League (UDL). Jemison and Scott went to radio station WLCS and announced a citywide bus boycott to begin on June 20. They advocated that all African Americans to stay off the buses and promised free rides to boycott participants. By the end of the following day, no black passengers rode the buses. The UDL held mass meetings at various locations in Baton Rouge, collecting money to fund a free ride system. While the boycott went on, black and white leaders continued to work on negotiating a settlement.

After several days of meetings, the two groups of leaders reached an agreement known as Ordinance 251. Under this ordinance, as under Ordinance 222, blacks would sit from the rear forward and whites from front to back. Blacks could not sit next to or in front of whites. To comply with the state's segregation laws, the two front sideways seats were always reserved for whites and the wide rear seat at the back of the bus was reserved for blacks.[33] Reverend Jemison announced the agreement on June 24, 1953, and although some blacks wanted to continue the boycott, the majority agreed to accept the compromise and end it.[34]

E. D. Nixon and Rosa Parks monitored the Baton Rouge boycott from Montgomery, and it became a model for the Montgomery boycott two years later. In the early stages of the Montgomery protest, Reverend Martin Luther King, Jr., called on Reverend Jemison for advice. In *Stride Toward Freedom*, his memoir of events in Montgomery, King wrote:

> knowing that Jemison and his associates had set up an effective private car pool, I put in a long-distance call to ask him for suggestions for a similar pool in Montgomery. As I expected, his painstaking description of the Baton Rouge experience was invaluable. I passed on word of...Jemison's advice to the transportation committee and suggested that we immediately begin setting up [a similar system].[35]

Rosa Parks herself regarded the Baton Rouge effort as an attempt to vindicate Homer Plessy, who in 1892 had challenged Jim Crow railroad car segregation but lost his case in the U.S. Supreme Court.[36]

However, E. D. Nixon was doing more than simply monitoring Baton Rouge's boycott. Over the years, he tried to negotiate policy changes with the bus company. On one occasion, he met with company officials to end the practice of blacks being required to pay at the front door, exit the bus, and board through the rear door. The company officials claimed that African Americans started the practice and wanted to keep it. Another time Nixon wanted the company to extend the Day Street bus route so that blacks who lived across the Day Street Bridge would not have to walk half a mile to a bus stop. The bus company refused, telling him that as long as people were willing to walk, the company would not extend service.[37] As an individual, Nixon could not force the company to make changes. That would only come with organization and community support.

Nevertheless, the tide was slowly turning against segregation, at least at the national level. Less than one year after the Baton Rouge boycott, the U.S. Supreme Court began dismantling Jim Crow segregation with its *Brown v. Board of Education* decision. In a unanimous decision read on May 17, 1954, Chief Justice Earl Warren declared

> that in the field of public education the doctrine of "separate but equal" has no place.... Separate educational facilities are inherently unequal.... To separate them [black children] from others of similar age and qualifications solely because of their race generates a feeling of inferiority as to their status in the community that may affect their hearts and minds in a way unlikely ever to be undone.[38]

One year later, the court implemented guidelines that gave federal district courts the power to supervise school desegregation with "all deliberate speed."[39] Although some school districts decided to comply with the law, resistance by many whites was swift. School boards across the south closed public schools, only to reopen them as private schools. In Mississippi, racists organized the White Citizen's Council, a vigilante group modeled on the KKK, which quickly spread across the region. Southern congressmen issued their Southern Manifesto, arguing that

> the decisions of the Supreme Court in the school cases [was] a clear abuse of judicial power. It climaxes a trend in the Federal Judiciary undertaking to legislate, in derogation of the authority of Congress, and to encroach upon the reserved rights of the States and the people.... We decry the Supreme Court's encroachment on the rights reserved to the States and to the people, contrary to established law, and to the Constitution. We commend the motives of those States which have declared the intention to resist forced integration by any lawful means.[40]

In early 1956, the governors of South Carolina, Georgia, Mississippi, and Virginia pressed other southern states to declare that the
federal government had no power to prohibit segregation and to "protest in appropriate language, against the encroachment of the central
government upon the sovereignty of the states and their people."[41]
Nevertheless, African Americans saw *Brown* as a gigantic step forward.
According to Rosa Parks,

> You can't imagine the rejoicing among black people, and some
> white people, when the Supreme Court decision came down in
> May 1954. The Court had said that separate education could not
> be equal, and many of us saw how the same idea applied to other
> things, like public transportation.[42]

Other court rulings specifically targeted transportation issues. In
1950, the U.S. Supreme Court ruled in *Henderson v. US* that racial
segregation on interstate railway dining cars was "an undue burden on
interstate commerce." Writing for the majority, Justice Burton said,

> Under the rules of an interstate railroad, dining cars are divided so
> as to allot ten tables exclusively to white passengers and one table
> exclusively to Negro passengers, and a curtain separates the table
> reserved for Negroes from the others. Under these rules, only four
> Negro passengers may be served at one time and then only at the
> table reserved for Negroes. Other Negroes who present themselves
> are compelled to await a vacancy at that table, although there
> may be many vacancies elsewhere in the diner....Held: These
> rules and practices violate 3 (1) of the Interstate Commerce Act,
> which makes it unlawful for a railroad in interstate commerce
> "to subject any particular person...to any undue or unreasonable
> prejudice or disadvantage in any respect whatsoever."[43]

After this ruling, African Americans traveling by railway had little
or no difficulty in obtaining nonsegregated first-class accommodations.
Further, in 1955, the Interstate Commerce Commission declared that
all segregation on interstate trains and buses, including waiting rooms,
would end by January 10, 1956. Southern states began to comply,

however reluctantly; but since the ICC decision applied to only *inter-state* travel, some states established separate waiting rooms for black passengers traveling within state lines.[44]

Despite these gains, the pace toward black equality was slow and un-even. In many southern states, segregationists singled out black organi-zations for attack. Since the NAACP had led the fight for integration, it became a target for attack. By 1956, using legal means, several states, in effect, stopped NAACP operations and forced the closure of local chapters. In Louisiana, courts granted a ban that ended all NAACP meetings until the organization filed a complete list of its members with the secretary of state. In South Carolina, legislators called for the NAACP's classification as a subversive organization. An Arkansas congressman entered into the *Congressional Record* 40 pages of "evi-dence" that NAACP officers and leading members were un-American. In Alabama, local judges barred NAACP activities when the orga-nization refused to release a list of its members. The NAACP sued and the Alabama State Circuit Court found that the organization had violated the state's constitution and laws. Therefore the court perma-nently barred the NAACP from doing business in the state. The case eventually found its way to the U.S. Supreme Court. In a unanimous decision, the Court found that the state had violated the due process clause of the Fourteenth Amendment and "a compelled disclosure of the NAACP's membership lists would have the effect of suppressing legal association among the group's members. Nothing short of an "overriding valid interest of the State," something not present in this case, "was needed to justify Alabama's actions."[45] Meanwhile white ter-rorism was on the rise. In 1956, when the federal government ordered the state of Alabama to admit Autherine Lucy, a black student, to the University of Alabama, students and local residents turned to violence to prevent her from attending the university. When rioting broke out, university officials suspended Lucy from the university. She then ac-cused officials of conspiring to keep her out of the university, leading the board of regents to expel her.[46]

Yet despite the setbacks, Rosa Parks remembered this period as a time of hope and ferment, as African Americans came to believe that segregation could be overthrown.[47] In the year between the *Brown* decision and the Supreme Court's implementation decision, black and white racial activists began making plans. It was also during this time that Rosa Parks became acquainted with Clifford and Virginia Durr. This relationship propelled Rosa Parks's activism forward once again.

The Durrs, who were white, were an anomaly in the Jim Crow South. Clifford Durr, born and raised in Montgomery, Alabama, was the son of a wealthy businessman. After graduating from the University of Alabama, he won a Rhodes scholarship to study at Oxford University in England, graduating in 1922 with a law degree. Returning to Montgomery, he passed the bar exam and accepted a position in a prestigious Birmingham law firm. In 1926, Clifford Durr married Virginia Foster, a well-educated daughter of a Presbyterian minister. During the Great Depression, Clifford Durr accepted a job in Washington, D.C., with the Reconstruction Finance Corporation, a New Deal agency created to ensure the survival of large banks, railroads, farm mortgage associations, savings and loan associations, and life insurance companies. He later joined the Federal Communications Commission (FCC) but became involved in conflicts there as well with the House Un-American Activities Committee (HUAC) and the Federal Bureau of Investigation (FBI) over civil liberties issues. Virginia Durr, meanwhile, became a founding member of the Southern Conference for Human Welfare (SCHW). Although drawn to the group primarily because of her interest in ending the poll tax, Virginia became interested in labor union issues and civil rights. In 1941, Virginia became the vice-president of the SCHW's civil rights committee, later renamed the National Committee to Abolish the Poll Tax (NCAPT). In 1951, the Durrs returned to Montgomery, but their lives had been forever changed by their experiences in Washington. Their exposure to New Deal liberals had broadened their world and they began to see southern society from a new perspective. Both Clifford and Virginia now viewed southern racial mores and American justice with a healthy skepticism.[48]

In this postwar period of red baiting and McCarthyism, many progressive and liberal groups were publicly attacked by conservatives for alleged Communist associations, and in fact both the SCHW and the NCAPT did occasionally receive financial support from a variety of Communist-backed organizations. Moreover, a few members were associated with the Communist Party, USA, but the NCAPT accepted donations from anyone opposed to the poll tax, no matter their political affiliation. Anti-Communist activists often targeted the Durrs because they were active in both groups. In 1954, Senator James O. Eastland (D-MS) subpoenaed Virginia Durr to testify before his Internal Security Committee, a commission similar to HUAC, about her work with the Southern Educational Fund (SEF), a supposed "subversive" organization. Durr refused to answer any questions, often taking out her compact and powdering her nose while the committee peppered her with questions. It was only the intervention of Texas Senator Lyndon B. Johnson, a friend from the Durrs' New Deal years, that ended the harassment of Eastland and his committee. Nevertheless, the damage had been done. Clifford Durr suffered a nervous collapse, and all his hopes for a successful legal practice died. However, Virginia found the hearings liberating. "In a way," she recalled, "I was glad my cover as a nice, proper Southern lady was blown by the hearing, because...I could begin to say what I really thought."[49] After his recovery, Clifford and Virginia worked with African Americans in Montgomery on civil rights and civil liberties cases. E. D. Nixon, then president of the Montgomery NAACP, brought Clifford Durr many cases. According to Virginia Durr, "they didn't pay much, but still he brought them to us." Financially, the Durrs scraped by, often receiving donations from liberal philanthropists they met during their years in Washington.[50]

In her autobiography, Virginia recalled that "Mr. Nixon was a very nice man and we liked him a lot. He was an honest, forthright kind of fellow." However, no matter how much Virginia liked Nixon or Nixon liked Virginia, in public the rules of southern racial etiquette had to be followed. One day she saw Nixon at the post office and said, "Why, hello Ed....He didn't say anything. I held out my hand and said, "Hello, Ed," and he didn't take my hand."[51] Nixon knew he could never refer to Virginia Durr by her first name, nor could he shake her hand in public. Later Nixon told her, "Look, don't you ever call me Ed again. If I called you Virginia, I'd be lynched....You ought to have better sense than to come up to a black man in the public post office and say 'Hello, Ed' and put out your hand." Virginia recalled that Rosa Parks was different, too. "I couldn't call her Rosa until she could call me Virginia....I had to call them Mrs. or Mr. until they could call me by my first name."[52]

The Durrs, E. D. Nixon, and Rosa Parks developed a very strong relationship. Both E. D. Nixon and Rosa Parks kept the Durrs informed about what was going on in the NAACP in Montgomery. Virginia Durr remembered that after the *Brown* decision, Rosa Parks was one of the people who helped black schoolchildren, tutoring them and making sure they were properly dressed and received their schoolbooks. Virginia recalled,

> She didn't have an automobile, so she rode the bus. She made only twenty-three dollars a week as a seamstress at the Montgomery Fair...a big department store here. Mrs. Parks's husband worked as a barber and he was sometimes sick and unemployed. They lived in a housing project with her mother, who kept house for them.

Rosa Parks supplemented her meager income by doing extra sewing, but Virginia Durr claimed she never charged enough for her work. "I used to be embarrassed at the amount she charged to make a dress. She'd charge, say three dollars, which was absurd."[53] Rosa Parks, according to Virginia Durr, was a hardworking, honest, and proud woman.

In early summer of 1955, Virginia Durr received a letter from Myles Horton, cofounder of the Highlander Folk School. Horton had a two-week scholarship available and wanted Virginia to find someone in Montgomery, preferably somebody black, to come to Highlander to attend a workshop. Virginia Durr "immediately thought of Mrs. Parks. It was the summer before the boycott."[54]

NOTES

1. "History of the NAACP," http://www.naacp.org/about/history/timeline/index.htm (accessed July 27, 2009).

2. John Hope Franklin and Alfred A. Moss, *From Slavery to Freedom*, 8th ed. (New York: McGraw Hill, 2000), 481.

3. Douglas Brinkley, *Rosa Parks; A Life* (New York: Penguin Books, 2000), 63–64; Rosa Parks with Jim Haskins, *My Story* (New York: Penguin Books, 1992), 93; Harry S. Truman Library and Museum, http://www.trumanlibrary.org/whistlestop/study_collections/desegregation/large/index.php (accessed August 1, 2009).

4. Herbert Shapiro, *White Violence and Black Response* (Cambridge, MA: University of Massachusetts Press, 1988), 373.

5. Ibid.

6. Kathy Lohr, "FBI Re-Examines 1946 Lynching Case," http://www.npr.org/templates/story/story.php?storyId=5579862 (accessed August 1, 2009).

7. Shapiro, *White Violence and Black Response*, 373; Lohr, "FBI Re-Examines 1946 Lynching Case."

8. Parks, *My Story*, 92.

9. Ibid., 93.

10. Shapiro, *White Violence and Black Response*, 373.

11. David McCullough, *Truman* (New York: Simon & Schuster, 1992), 570.

12. Ibid.

13. Ibid., 587.

14. "End of U.S. Military Segregation Set Stage for Rights Movement," http://www.america.gov/st/peopleplace-english/2008/February/20080225120859liameruoy0.9820215.html (accessed August 1, 2009).

15. McCullough, *Truman*, 724.

16. Ibid., 588.

17. Gerald N. Rosenberg, *The Hollow Hope: Can Courts Bring About Social Change?* 2nd ed. (Chicago: University of Chicago Press, 2008), 154.

18. Vivian M. Baulch and Patricia Zacharias, "The 1943 Detroit Race Riots," *Detroit News*, http://apps.detnews.com/apps/history/index.php?id=185 (accessed August 3, 2009).

19. Ibid.

20. Ibid.

21. Brinkley, *Rosa Parks*, 67.

22. Ibid., 68.

23. Parks, *My Story*, 89; Brinkley, *Rosa Parks*, 69–70.

24. Joanne Grant, *Ella Baker: Freedom Bound* (New York: John Wiley & Sons, 1998), 7–24.

25. Ibid., 73.

26. Lynne Olson, *Freedom's Daughters: The Unsung Heroines of the Civil Rights Movement from 1830 to 1970* (New York: Scribner, 2002), 74.

27. Brinkley, *Rosa Parks*, 71.

28. Parks, *My Story*, 94.

29. "The Baton Rouge Bus Boycott of 1953 ... A Recaptured Past," http://www.lib.lsu.edu/special/exhibits/boycott/ (accessed August 3, 2009).

30. Mary Price, "Baton Rouge Bus Boycott Background," http://www.lib.lsu.edu/special/exhibits/boycott/background.html (accessed August 4, 2009).

31. Ibid.

32. Ibid.

33. Veterans of the Civil Rights Movement, http://www.crmvet.org/tim/timhis53.htm (accessed August 4, 2009); Louisiana State Museum, http://lsm.crt.state.la.us/post-ed8.htm (accessed August 4, 2009).

34. Price, "Baton Rouge Bus Boycott Background."

35. Louisiana State Museum, http://lsm.crt.state.la.us/post-ed8.htm (accessed August 4, 2009).

36. Brinkley, *Rosa Parks*, 76.

37. Ruth Edmonds Hill, ed., *The Black Woman Oral History Project*, vol. 8 (Westport, CT: Meckler, 1991), 254; Parks, *My Story*, 108–9.

38. U.S. Supreme Court, *Brown v. Board of Education*, 347 U.S. 483 (1954), http://caselaw.lp.findlaw.com/scripts/getcase.pl?court=us&vol=347&invol=483 (accessed August 4, 2009).

39. U.S. Supreme Court, *Brown v. Board of Education*, 349 U.S. 294 (1955), http://caselaw.lp.findlaw.com/scripts/getcase.pl?court=US&vol=349&invol=294 (accessed August 4, 2009).

40. "The Southern Manifesto," *Congressional Record*, 84th Congress, Second Session, vol. 102, part 4 (March 12, 1956) (Washington, DC: Government Printing Office, 1956), 4459–60, http://www.strom.clemson.edu/strom/manifesto.html (accessed August 4, 2009).

41. Franklin and Moss, *From Slavery to Freedom*, 513.

42. Parks, *My Story*, 99–100.

43. U.S. Supreme Court, *Henderson v. United States*, 339 U.S. 816 (1950), http://laws.findlaw.com/us/339/816.html (accessed August 10, 2009).

44. Franklin and Moss, *From Slavery to Freedom*, 509.

45. U.S. Supreme Court, *NAACP v. Alabama*, 377 U.S. 288 (1964), http://laws.findlaw.com/us/377/288.html (accessed August 11, 2009);

NAACP v. Alabama, http://www.oyez.org/cases/1950–1959/1957/1957_91 (accessed August 11, 2009).

46. Franklin and Moss, *From Slavery to Freedom,* 514.

47. Parks, *My Story,* 100.

48. See Virginia Durr, *Outside the Magic Circle: The Autobiography of Virginia Foster Durr,* ed. Hollinger F. Barnard (Birmingham: University of Alabama Press, 1985); Sarah Hart Brown, *Standing Against Dragons: Three Southern Lawyers in a Era of Fear* (Baton Rouge: Louisiana State University Press, 1998); Patricia Sullivan, ed., *Freedom Writer: Virginia Foster Durr, Letters from the Civil Rights Years* (New York: Routledge, 2003).

49. Sullivan, *Freedom Writer,* 31.

50. See Durr, *Outside the Magic Circle;* Sullivan, *Freedom Writer.*

51. Durr, *Outside the Magic Circle,* 252.

52. Ibid., 252–53.

53. Ibid., 278.

54. Ibid.

Chapter 5

THE FOUNDATIONS OF
THE BOYCOTT

As African Americans stepped up their efforts to achieve first-class citizenship, the Highlander Folk School created three major programs to both encourage and strengthen these efforts. In the fall of 1932, Myles Horton and Don West originally founded Highlander Folk School in the mountains of Tennessee as a center "for the training of labor leaders."[1] Between 1932 and the mid-1940s, Highlander's programs worked with woodcutters, coal miners, government relief workers, textile workers, and farmers in the region to build a progressive labor movement. The staff supported strikes and organizing drives and trained workers to take leadership in labor unions. During this period, Horton worked with labor activists to develop a residential educational program intended to build an expansive, racially integrated, and politically active southern labor movement. By 1948, both blacks and whites took part in Highlander's programs and the school's newsletter was writing about "Highlander's Program in Civil Rights."[2] Horton decided that it was time to do something about racism, and the staff believed that the best way to approach the problem was "to get people together and trust that the solution would arise from them."[3]

Beginning in 1953, Horton organized a series of workshops on the United Nations, but the people who came to Highlander that year reshaped the program to address the issues that were most important to them. Some of the first participants came from the Sea Islands of South Carolina. One man, Esau Jenkins from Johns Island, owned a restaurant and motel and ran a bus for the black people on the island who worked as domestics in Charleston. On his trips between Johns Island and Charleston, Jenkins tried to teach his passengers to read well enough to pass the literacy test required for voter registration. Like many African Americans at this time, Jenkins understood the importance of the vote for achieving first-class citizenship rights and equality. Although a few people did pass the test, Jenkins knew that the 30-minute trip was too short to do very much. When Jenkins arrived at Highlander, he told Horton and the Highlander staff that he was not really interested in the United Nations; he wanted to get teachers to help the African Americans on Johns Island learn to read so that they could vote. Another participant, Septima Clark, a teacher from Charleston, was interested in Jenkins's program. Together, Jenkins, Clark, and Horton worked to help the people of Johns Island become literate. Over the years, Citizenship Schools, led by local residents, spread throughout the South and taught local people that they could make a difference at home and by extension help change the world.[4]

One month after the U.S. Supreme Court handed down the *Brown v. Board of Education* decision, Highlander Folk School held its second summer workshop on desegregation of the public schools. Southern educators, as well as the Highlander staff, were hopeful that a new cooperative effort would improve education for all children in the South. Black and white teachers and parents came from South Carolina, Alabama, Georgia, and Tennessee to develop "a program of action directly related to the needs of each community."[5] A third workshop in the summer of 1955 brought together previous participants who had returned home to involve others in their community as well as a new cadre of local activists. A brochure distributed by the planning committee stated that eligible attendees included anyone working with local "educational, religious, fraternal, or intercultural organizations or otherwise in a position to provide community leadership."[6] There were no educational requirements and Highlander made scholarships available so people of many educational and economic backgrounds could participate. When Myles Horton contacted Virginia Durr in the summer of 1955 about sending a local activist from Montgomery, she immediately recommended Rosa Parks.

Virginia Durr asked Rosa Parks if she would like to go to Highlander to attend the workshop, since Horton was offering a scholarship. Rosa told her that she would like to go, but she just did not have the $12 or $15 for the round-trip bus fare to Monteagle, Tennessee. "If I can get you some money, can you go?" Durr asked. Durr told Rosa that she would ask Aubrey Williams, a former New Deal administrator and civil rights activist, for the money. According to Durr, "It was painful for her. She was a very proud woman.... But Mrs. Parks was very fond of Aubrey Williams. By this time she was fond of me, too, and she really wanted to go."[7] Writing to Highlander's executive secretary, Mrs. Henry F. Shipherd, Rosa said,

This is to say that I accept with sincere appreciation the scholarship for the Desegregation Workshop. The registration card is enclosed. I am certainly most grateful to Mrs. Durr for recommending me to you.... The Highlander Folk School seems like a wonderful place. I am looking forward with eager anticipation to attending the workshop, hoping to make a contribution to the fulfillment of a complete freedom for all people.[8]

So Rosa Parks boarded a bus and arrived at Highlander for a two-week workshop focused on implementing the *Brown* decision.

The workshop sessions centered on group discussion of common problems faced by African Americans from different areas. Highlander staff and consultants took part in the process, but overall the community people who led the discussions. Each local leader described his or her community and its problems to the group. The group then worked to identify and analyze the common problems of the various communities represented in the workshop. In this way, each participant learned from the others and in the process gained a broader perspective on racial problems as well as what had been accomplished elsewhere. Finally, as a group, the participants worked to develop practical plans and guidelines for action at home. Rosa Parks kept detailed notes of the workshop discussions. In her personal handwritten notes on the Social Action Program developed at Highlander, she wrote that everyone who wishes to participate should be encouraged to do so, but the community "Policy [should be] not to use persons with [a] record of trouble with [the] law. Give them something to do where they will not be in forefront of action." In addition, "People should be, as far as possible, economically independent. Not to owe too many debts, or borrow money from certain places."[9] Character counted.

Other participants recalled that at first, Rosa Parks was "extremely shy and quiet." However, Rosa recalled that within a few days, she adjusted to the notion of working on important problems in informal discussion groups and was sufficiently relaxed and comfortable to able to participate freely in workshops with others working toward the same goals. The Highlander workshop was an eye-opening experience for blacks and whites alike. For many, this was the first time they had ever interacted with the opposite race based on complete equality. Not only did the participants attend workshops together, they interacted socially as well. One white couple that had limited contact with blacks stated that the most important experience for them was getting to know African Americans not just in workshops but "in the kitchen, washing dishes together." This was a revelation for blacks as well. One African American attendee wrote, "It was the first time I ever worked in a kitchen where I was in charge and a white man was doing the dishes!" Workshops at Highlander gave all participants an experience in "democratic living in practice." As Esau Jenkins wrote, "It was very significant and exclamatory to me to find democracy at work in Monteagle at Highlander Folk School which place makes me feel that he is counted as a human being, and one of God's people."[10] Rosa Parks recalled that at Highlander, everyone shared not only in the workshops and fellowship but also in the mundane housekeeping tasks that were posted each day. She took pleasure in the unwonted experience of having whites prepare her breakfast, cooking for whites and blacks alike, and in an atmosphere in which racism and hostility were notable by their absence. She could speak freely without fearing retribution or antagonism.[11] The Highlander experience was the most liberating of her life, but when Horton asked the participants what they were going to do about segregation when the got home, Rosa said, "I really can't say that I'll do anything because I just don't see anything that can be done."[12]

Rosa Parks maintained her ties to the Highlander School and the wider civil rights movement. In October 1988, a room at the Martin Luther King Center in Atlanta was dedicated to her. On that occasion, she linked hands and sang with Coretta Scott King, center, and Highlander founder and director Myles Horton. (AP Photo)

Highlander also reacquainted Rosa Parks and Ella Baker, NAACP director of branches, when Baker led one of the sessions. However, according to Rosa Parks's recollections, Septima Poinsette Clark, another black woman activist she met at Highlander, most impressed her. Clark, the daughter of a freedman and freeborn black mother grew up dedicated to the one thing both her parents valued: education. She recalled, "The only thing I remember that my father would whip you for was if you didn't want to go to school."[13] After Clark graduated from Avery Institute, she looked for a job teaching, but at that time, the Charleston public school system did not allow African Americans to teach. However, a school on Johns Island, one of the many Sea Islands off the coast of South Carolina, did need a teacher. Clark began her teaching career in the midst of rural desperation. The black population of the island lived in virtual slavery, either working in the fields for whites or traveling to Charleston to work as domestics. After three years on Johns Island, Clark accepted a teaching position at Avery Institute and later moved on to teach in McClellanville, Johns Island again, and Columbia. Like most African American teachers in the South, Clark had to deal with inadequate schoolhouses, lack of student transportation, short school terms, and overcrowded classrooms, and low wages. In 1916, Clark received $35 per month as principal and teacher, and a second teacher received $25 for instructing a class of more than 60 students. In comparison, white teachers taught classes with no more than 18 students, and they were paid $85 per month.[14] The inequality appalled Clark, so she and several other teachers worked with NAACP lawyer Thurgood Marshall to prepare a 1945 court case to force the Columbia public school system to equalize black and white teachers' salaries. She later said:

> My participation in this fight...was what might be described by some...as my first "radical" job. I would call it my first effort in a social action challenging the status quo...I felt that in reality I was working for the accomplishment of something that ultimately would be good for everyone.[15]

The court decided that teacher salaries must be equal; as a result, school authorities required teachers to take a national exam. Clark took the exam, received an A, and her salary tripled. Then, in 1956, South Carolina passed a statute that prohibited city employees from joining civil rights organizations, and the school board fired Clark because she refused to resign from the NAACP. Clark worked to mobilize other black teachers to strike against the law, but she was unsuccessful. Nearly 30 years later, Clark saw these attempts as "one of the failures of my life, because I tried to push them into something they weren't ready for.... That taught me a good lesson." An outside leader, Clark learned, could not dictate social change—a community must be "ready from within."[16]

Clark had attended and directed workshops at Highlander in 1954 and was influential at Highlander even before she became a member of the staff. When the school board fired her in 1956, Myles Horton immediately offered Clark a job. Within two years, she became the director of the integration workshops at Highlander and then director of the Citizenship School program. Citizenship Schools were committed to promoting literacy and political empowerment in African American communities. Highlander-trained local residents became teachers and worked with other community members, teaching them to write their names, balance a checkbook, fill out a voter ballot, and understand their rights and responsibilities as American citizens. Clark developed a method of teaching based on relating subjects like math and English to the kinds of problems people faced in everyday life. She would teach adults to read by beginning with street signs and newspapers. Clark wrote, "I just thought that you couldn't get people to register and vote until you teach them to read and write."[17] For Clark, there was an undeniable link between education and political rights. Horton recalled that Clark's workshop methods differed greatly from his—"she was less interested in asking questions…[she] relied on materials. I was trying to help people learn, she was trying to teach people….Her approach was much more popular than mine."[18]

Rosa Parks once said that her mother was her greatest influence because of her deep moral and philosophical commitment to social justice. Leona McCauley always told her daughter to "treat others as I wished to be treated" and to expect the same in return.[19] In Septima Clark, Rosa Parks found another African American woman who served as a role model of civil rights activism. Clark had overcome great obstacles, fought for equal education and equal pay, and lost her job because of her membership in the NAACP. While Clark was at Highlander, the local police frequently raided and harassed the school. In one such raid, the police arrested Clark—a well-known teetotaler—and charged her with selling liquor. However, Clark knew "integration was what really worried them." Segregationists, state officials, and local law enforcement believed Highlander to be a hotbed of Communist activity. Clark said, "anyone who was against segregation was called a communist. White southerners couldn't believe that a southerner could have the idea of racial equality; they thought it had to come from somewhere else."[20] In 1959, after an investigation by the Tennessee legislature, police officers raided and closed Highlander. A state judge revoked Highlander's charter and confiscated its property on the grounds that Highlander had sold liquor without a license. Law enforcement padlocked the buildings, and nightriders burned them to the ground. Undeterred, two years later Myles Horton found a loophole in a state law that allowed him to get a new charter. He reopened Highlander in 1961 in the Bay Mountains 20 miles east of Knoxville.[21] Recalling her time at Highlander and Septima Clark, Rosa Parks said,

> I am always very respectful and very much in awe of the presence of Septima Clark, because her life story makes the effort

that I have made very minute. I only hope that there is a possible chance that some of her great courage and dignity and wisdom has rubbed off on me.[22]

Rosa Parks wrote that she did not know what she would do to end segregation when she returned to Montgomery after 10 days at Highlander. In her autobiography she expressed her reluctance to leave, knowing that on her return to Montgomery, she would once again have to take up her work at the Montgomery Fair department store and submit, politely and with a smile, to all its accompanying indignities. Moreover, she would again be subject to the daily trials of traveling to and from work on the city's segregated buses.[23] Yet, as a civil rights activist and an active member of the NAACP, Rosa Parks had to be aware of the growing discontent with Jim Crow segregation in Montgomery. She certainly knew of E. D. Nixon's forays to the bus company to register complaints about the treatment African Americans received on city buses. She would have had to be aware of the actions of other activists in Montgomery as well. She kept track of segregation cases, newspaper articles, and wrote reports detailing cases for the Montgomery NAACP. It would be impossible for Rosa Parks to have missed the ways that African Americans were mounting challenges to Jim Crow, especially those challenges brought forward by other African American women—women who distinguished themselves through their perseverance and abilities to meet the challenges that faced them every day. Conscious of the injustices of racism, African American women often initiated activities aimed at social change and empowerment.

Rosa Parks once wrote that blacks in Montgomery were more angered by the bus segregation laws than by any other aspect of Jim Crow. The city's 50,000 African Americans formed the majority of the bus ridership, since whites were better able to afford to buy cars. She wrote with particular bitterness about the week-in, week-out humiliation of riding segregated buses in order to "go downtown and work for white people."[24] It was not just working-class blacks who suffered these indignities on public transportation—Jim Crow segregation statutes allowed no exceptions because of socioeconomic status, education, or occupation. All African Americans were subject to the same rules, but not all African Americans followed the same path in seeking racial equality. While Rosa Parks worked with the NAACP and participated in workshops at Highlander Folk School, other black women organized a separate women's group to attack segregation in Montgomery.

Mary Fair Burks organized the Women's Political Council in Montgomery as a result of the racism she experienced as well as her desire to motivate black middle-class women to take action to change segregated Montgomery. Burks knew that all African Americans could recall painful incidents that introduced them to the racial climate in the South. For her it was when some whites called her brother a "nigger" and he rushed into the house to get his BB gun so that he could kill them. Burks wrote that until that moment, she had never heard that word, nor was she aware of differences in skin color, and she was devastated when her mother explained the "facts of life" to her. "I also remember being abruptly jerked from the front seat of a bus by my mother who, fiercely gripping my hand, took me to the back, where I stood." Then she learned about "White" and "Colored" water fountains, rest rooms, trains, and restaurants. "The more I learned the more bitter I became," she later wrote. She was so angry, Burks said, that she began her own "private guerilla warfare," entering rest rooms that were designated "For White Ladies Only," or ignoring elevators clearly marked "For Whites Only." Once, the police almost arrested her for walking through a "Whites Only" park. Burks left Montgomery to attend graduate school at the University of Michigan, finding Ann Arbor "almost Eden. . . . For the first time since I had learned about segregation, I knew what it meant to feel and live like a whole human being." Like Rosa Parks after her experience at Highlander, Burks found it more difficult to return to Montgomery and accept the status quo. "When I cam back to Montgomery," she wrote, "I was even more embittered by its unrelenting racism."[25]

Then an incident occurred that resulted in Burks's arrest. She was in her car behind a bus when the traffic light turned green. As she began to accelerate, she saw a white woman attempting to get to the curb. The woman began cursing at Burks for accelerating before she had reached the curb. Then police arrived and arrested Burks. Burks tried to explain that it was the white woman using profanity, not her, but the police officer did not want to listen to her. He hit her with his nightstick and threw her in a jail cell. Burks's husband arrived at the jail with a family friend and a white lawyer who read the charges, tore them up, and demanded her release. For Burks, this incident was the catalyst for an organized effort "to do something more about segregation."[26]

The following Sunday, inspired by a sermon by Pastor Vernon Johns of the Dexter Avenue Baptist Church, Burks decided to get the women she knew together to address racial problems. She knew that they too had suffered racial abuse and indignity, all African Americans had. "Thus the idea of the Women's Political Council was born on that Sunday morning following my arrest." During the following week, she contacted 50 women; most were professional women—educators, supervisors, principals, teachers, and social workers—about organizing a group to address some of the city's racial issues. To her surprise, 40 women attended the first organizational meeting in the fall of 1946.[27] As Burks had instinctively known, every woman at the meeting could recall a degrading racial incident, and all agreed to work to achieve political leverage and protest racial abuses.

> We finally agreed on a three-tier approach: first, political action, including voter registration and interviewing candidates for office; second, protest about abuses on city buses and use of taxpayer's money to operate segregated parks (we assumed that segregated schools and housing would be with us forever, and they still are); third, education, which involved teaching young high school students about democracy and how it was intended to operate as well as teaching adults to read and write well enough to fulfill the literacy requirements for voting.[28]

Long before Highlander began its Citizenship Schools, African American women were aware of the power of the vote and the necessity of literacy training for adults to achieve political power.

In 1946, very few African Americans had registered to vote in Montgomery, and these middle-class, well-educated women were no exception. Even though they were well educated, the literacy test had prevented many of them from registering. According to Burks, "Even Ph.D.s failed the test, since Negroes could never be sure of minor details such as their precinct number, which was changed arbitrarily without notification." While the WPC members worked on becoming registered voters, they began organizing citywide registration schools that met weekly in various churches as well. Black men and women who attended the classes learned to fill out registration forms and, if necessary, how to write. WPC members accompanied the participants to courthouses, when they attempted to register, and then again when they returned to check their results. In addition, the WPC worked with the League of Women Voters to have white candidates speak to black voters about issues and policies. Then the WPC, working with other black organizations, came up with a list of candidates whom they recommended for bloc voting. Using this strategy, the WPC helped African American voters to decide the outcomes in close political races.[29]

Other programs included simulating the workings of city government with black high school students through a two-day program that taught black students the duties and responsibilities of city officials as well as what democracy should mean. Burks recalled that many of the students who participated in the program registered to vote as soon as they became 21 (the legal age for voting at that time), became active in politics, and later some went on to become lawyers, judges, and state legislators. The WPC also met with the Montgomery park commission to point out that African Americans paid taxes to maintain the parks but then segregation laws prohibited blacks from using them. The WPC made little headway with the commission. The only concession the commission made was to allow blacks to walk through the parks on their way to work for whites.[30]

Meanwhile, the WPC attacked the issue of abuses on the city buses. Almost daily, a black patron had an unpleasant experience on a bus. Police arrested Mrs. Geneva Johnson for not having correct change and "talking back" to the driver when he reprimanded her. Mrs. Johnson paid a fine for disorderly conduct but kept riding the bus. E. D. Nixon, sometimes alone, sometimes with a group of African American men, complained to the bus company about these incidents, but nothing changed. Later, police arrested Mrs. Viola White and Miss Katie Wingfield as well as two children, Edwina Johnson and her brother Marshall, visiting from New Jersey, for sitting in the front seats reserved for whites.[31] All paid a fine, and African Americans kept riding the buses. JoAnn Robinson, a professor of English at Alabama State University, boarded a city bus in 1949 and dropped her coins in the fare box.

Distracted, she sat in the fifth row of the almost empty bus, and closed
her eyes. Hearing someone shouting, she looked up and noticed that
the driver had stopped the bus. "If you can sit in the fifth row from the
front of other buses in Montgomery, suppose you get off and ride in one
of them," the driver shouted. When Mrs. Robinson, still distracted did
not respond, the driver came and stood over her. He raised his hand to
strike her, yelling "Get up from there!" She leapt to her feet and ran to
get off the bus.[32] Socioeconomic status, education, or occupation could
not protect African Americans from humiliation. In 1952, a white bus
driver and an intoxicated black man, Mr. Brooks, had a disagreement
about a dime the man had used to pay his fare. The driver called the police, and no one seems to know exactly what happened, but the police
shot and killed Mr. Brooks as he was getting off the bus. The coroner
ruled it a case of "justifiable homicide" because Brooks "resisted arrest."
In 1953, Mrs. Epsie Worthy boarded a bus at a transfer point, but the
driver refused to accept her transfer and demanded an additional fare.
Mrs. Worthy decided to walk the rest of the way rather than pay another fare. Nevertheless, the driver insisted she pay the additional fare
even if she decided to walk. The driver and Mrs. Worthy had words,
and as she stepped off the bus, the driver began to beat her. Mrs. Worthy defended herself, and when the police arrived, they arrested and
jailed her. The court fined her $52 for disorderly conduct. In 1953, the
WPC received more than 30 complaints against the bus company from
African Americans in Montgomery.[33] Clearly ending segregation on
the city buses was becoming a pressing issue.

By 1950, the WPC had grown to three chapters organized in three
sections of the city. JoAnn Robinson followed Mary Fair Burks as president of the main chapter of the WPC. Robinson called Mayor W. A.
Gayle and requested a meeting with him and the city commissioners to
discuss racial issues. The mayor promptly agreed to the meeting. Robinson recalled that the mayor was a very pleasant person and seemed
sincere in working with the WPC to overcome the problems of black
people. The WPC suggested actions to end nuisance problems and the
mayor and commissioners often accepted their ideas. According to
Robinson, "This relationship, when the WPC worked amicably with
the mayor's office, existed for several years. Only when the struggle
for integration on buses began did the friendship end. No longer did

members of the WPC attend city hall meetings, for that privilege was no longer offered."[34]

The WPC was not the only group in Montgomery working to end the segregated seating system on city buses. The Progressive Democratic Association, led by E. D. Nixon, and the Citizen's Steering Committee, headed by Rufus Lewis, tried to meet with the bus company to complain about the system and the behavior of some of the bus drivers, to no avail. After these efforts failed, the WPC attempted to meet with bus company officials, and again their efforts failed. At the same time, several local ministers, including Dr. Martin Luther King, Jr., had scheduled a meeting with the mayor and city council to discuss the situation. When Robinson called King, he invited three members of the WPC to join the meeting. This group presented written and signed reports to the city commission detailing past incidents, and the commission promised an immediate investigation. In the meantime, some African Americans, particularly men, began walking rather than riding the buses.

Shortly after this meeting, the bus company asked the city commissioners' permission to increase bus fares, since the number of riders was declining. The commissioners held a public meeting and WPC members and many others went to the meeting to protest. Black patrons did not object to the fare increase per se; rather, they voiced their displeasure with the type of service for which they had to pay. They presented a list of complaints, including discourteous treatment and the use of obscene language; fewer bus stops in black neighborhoods than in white neighborhoods; blacks paying in the front then being required to exit and enter the rear of the bus; and black riders being required to stand even if the front 10 seats reserved for whites were empty. After the hearings, the WPC did meet with J. H. Bagley, the bus company manager, as well. Bagley listened politely to the group, then told them that he was merely the manager and had no jurisdiction over the city government and its laws. The same WPC members also spoke to Mayor Gayle about the issues. The mayor explained that the laws were the laws and the bus drivers had to conform to the laws. He then suggested that if black patrons were upset, they could drive their own cars rather than ride the buses.[35] Of course, African Americans rode the buses because they did not own cars!

Nevertheless, Mayor Gayle asked the drivers to be more courteous, told the bus company to make stops at each block in the city and admit all passengers except those who had large packages at the front door. Then the mayor and commissioners approved the fare increase the company had requested and for a few days things improved. Buses stopped at each block and the drivers behaved more courteously. However, the changes were short-lived. Very quickly, the old ways returned. Black passengers were told to pay in front and go to the back to enter the bus; then the driver would pull away before they could board. When a young mother with two babies put her infants on the empty front seat while she paid her fare, the driver screamed at her and lunged the bus forward, throwing the babies into the aisle. The number of incidents mounted, complaints to the WPC increased, and the number of blacks walking rather than riding the buses grew.[36]

Then police arrested Claudette Colvin. Claudette was a quiet, well-mannered 15-year-old high school student who boarded the bus on March 2, 1955, and, with a few friends, sat in the colored section. Claudette, coming home from school, was carrying several textbooks so she could study for her exams. Blacks and whites crowded the bus, which was soon jammed with passengers, blacks and a few whites standing in the aisle. The driver demanded that the black passengers seated in the colored section move. At first no one responded, the bus was full and there was nowhere to go. The driver shouted at the black passengers again, and several apprehensive riders got off the bus and walked away. Slowly the seated black passengers stood up, all except for Claudette. The bus driver then stood over her and demanded that she give up her seat. Looking around, Claudette saw no empty seats, and she knew she was not in the first 19 rows reserved for whites. She remained seated, refusing to move. Claudette's teacher, Geraldine Nesbitt, had been teaching her class about black history and the Fourteenth Amendment, and Claudette had been emboldened by that history.[37] At the time of her arrest, Virginia Durr asked Claudette why she would not move. According to Durr, Claudette said, "I done paid my dime, they didn't have no *right* to move me."[38] In an interview with *Newsweek* in 2009, Claudette said, "I felt like Sojourner Truth was pushing down on one shoulder and Harriet Tubman was pushing down on the other— saying, 'Sit down girl!' I was glued to my seat."[39]

The enraged driver drove to town, calling a police officer to arrest Claudette. Two police officers entered the bus to make the arrest, commanding Claudette to stand. When she refused, they dragged her, kicking and screaming, off the bus. They forced her into a patrol car, handcuffed her, and drove her to jail. Police charged Claudette with misconduct, resisting arrest, and violating city segregation laws. African Americans and organizations began discussing a boycott. The WPC had already put a plan in place should the black community decide to boycott. They had fifty thousand notices ready to go; only the time and place needed to be added.

At first, many activists in Montgomery thought they had found their test case. Clifford Durr contacted Fred Gray, a young black attorney, to represent Claudette. In addition to being an A student, Claudette was a member of the NAACP Youth Council and her adviser was Rosa Parks, who taught the members to never lose their dignity. Claudette said that, "Mrs. Parks said always do what is right." According to historian Douglas Brinkley, Rosa Parks and Claudette's mother used to play together when they both lived in Pine Level, so Rosa "took a particular interest in the girl and her case."[40] The original plan was to negotiate a compromise seating plan on the buses based on a system in place in Mobile, Alabama. Blacks would fill the seats from back to front, whites from front to back; wherever they met was the dividing line. There was no outright call for the end of segregation, and Rosa Parks refused to support the plan or join in presenting the petition to the bus company and Montgomery officials. She wrote, "I didn't feel anything could be accomplished. I had decided that I would not go anywhere with a piece of paper in my hand asking white folks for any favors."[41] Rosa Parks, JoAnn Robinson, and E. D. Nixon did meet with Claudette about taking her case to federal court, began making plans to do so, and started raising money for her defense fund.[42] However, there were many opinions about Claudette Colvin's suitability as a catalyst for action. JoAnn Robinson wrote, "Some felt she was too young to be the trigger that precipitated a movement."[43] Claudette's sometimes unruly behavior and immature outbursts bothered Rosa Parks. However, when E. D. Nixon discovered that 15-year-old, unmarried Claudette Colvin was pregnant, that was the end of the case. Once the white press found out about her pregnancy, they would vilify her and the case would not have a chance. E. D. Nixon dropped the drive to press a legal case saying, "I had to be sure that I had somebody I could win with."[44]

In October, police arrested Mary Louise Smith, an 18-year-old for refusing to move to the rear of the bus. The incident was not publicized, and no one knew about it until after Smith's arrest and conviction. She paid her fine and continued to ride the buses.[45] However, Montgomery activists knew there was hope. In the spring of 1955, Sarah Mae Flemming sued the city bus company in Columbia, South Carolina, over the segregation statute. The U.S. Fourth Circuit Court of Appeals ruled that in Flemming's case, segregated seating was unconstitutional.[46] Therefore Montgomery activists knew that they could overturn the city's segregation ordinance; they just needed a plaintiff who was beyond reproach. The question was who?

NOTES

1. Aimee Isgrig Horton, *The Highlander Folk School: A History of Its Major Programs, 1932–1961* (New York: Carlson Publishing, 1989), 32.

2. Ibid., 186; Highlander Research and Education Center, http://www.highlandercenter.org/a-history.asp (accessed August 11, 2009).

3. Myles Horton, *The Long Haul: An Autobiography* (New York: Teachers College Press, 1998), 98.

4. Ibid., 99–104.

5. Horton, *The Highlander Folk School*, 202–3.

6. Ibid., 204.

7. Virginia Durr, *Outside the Magic Circle: The Autobiography of Virginia Foster Durr*, ed. Hollinger F. Barnard (Birmingham: University of Alabama Press, 1985), 278–79.

8. Douglas Brinkley, *Rosa Parks; A Life* (New York: Penguin Books, 2000), 93–94.

9. Horton, *The Highlander Folk School*, 205–7; Rosa Parks Papers, Wayne State University, Walter P. Reuther Library of Labor and Urban Affairs, box 2, folder 18, Highlander Folk School Meeting, 1955.

10. Horton, *The Highlander Folk School*, 208–9.

11. Rosa Parks, *My Story* (New York: Penguin Books, 1992), 105–6.

12. Dale Jacobs, *The Myles Horton Reader: Education for Social Change* (Knoxville: University of Tennessee Press, 2003), 38.

13. Eliot Wiggington, *Refuse to Stand Silently by: An Oral History of Grass Roots Social Activism in America, 1921–64* (New York: Doubleday, 1992).

14. Septima Clark and Cynthia Stokes Brown, *Ready from Within: A First Person Narrative* (Africa World Press; AWP ed., 1990); Septima Clark, *Echo in My Soul* (New York: E.P. Dutton and Co., 1962).

15. Clark, *Echo in My Soul*, 82.

16. Clark and Brown, *Ready from Within*.

17. Ibid.

18. Horton, *The Long Haul*, 103–5.

19. Rosa Parks Papers, Wayne State University, Walter P. Reuther Library of Labor and Urban Affairs, box 1, folder 3.

20. Clark and Brown, *Ready from Within*.

21. Highlander Research and Education Center, http://www.high landercenter.org/a-history.asp (accessed August 12, 2009); Tom Eblen, "Civil Rights Institution Fights for 'Economic Democracy,'" *Los Angeles Times* (November 26, 1982), D3.

22. Brinkley, *Rosa Parks*, 96–97.

23. Parks, *My Story*, 107.

24. Ibid., 108–9.

25. Mary Fair Burks, "Trailblazers: Women in the Montgomery Bus Boycott," in *Black Women in United States History*, ed. Darlene Clark Hine (New York: Carlson Publishing, 1990), 76.

26. Ibid., 78.

27. Ibid., 79; JoAnn Gibson Robinson, *The Montgomery Bus Boycott and the Women Who Started It* (Knoxville: University of Tennessee Press, 1987), 24.

28. Burks, "Trailblazers," 79.

29. Ibid., 80–81.

30. Ibid., 81.

31. Phillip Hoose, *Claudette Colvin: Twice Toward Justice* (Los Angeles: Farrar, Straus and Giroux, 2000), 8; Robinson, *The Montgomery Bus Boycott and the Women Who Started It*, 20–22.

32. Robinson, *The Montgomery Bus Boycott and the Women Who Started It*, 15–16.

33. Ibid., 20–22.

34. Ibid., 25.

35. Ibid., 31–32.

36. Ibid., 32–37.

37. Ibid., 37–38.

38. Patricia Sullivan, ed., *Freedom Writer: Virginia Foster Durr, Letters from the Civil Rights Years* (New York: Routledge, 2003), 84.

39. Eliza Gray, "A Forgotten Contribution," *Newsweek* (March 2, 2009).

40. Brinkley, *Rosa Parks*, 88.

41. Parks, *My Story*, 112.

42. Ibid.; Sullivan, *Freedom Writer*, 84.

43. Robinson, *The Montgomery Bus Boycott and the Women Who Started It*, 39.

44. Parks, *My Story*, 112; Brinkley, *Rosa Parks*, 90; Gray, "A Forgotten Contribution."

45. Robinson, *The Montgomery Bus Boycott and the Women Who Started It*, 43; Parks, *My Story*, 112.

46. *Sarah Mae Flemming, Appellant, v. South Carolina Electric and Gas Company, a Corporation, Appellee*, United States Court of Appeals Fourth Circuit.—224 F.2d 752, http://cases.justia.com/us-court-of-appeals/F2/224/752/145976/ (accessed August 14, 2009); South Carolina African American History Online, http://www.scafricanamerican.com/honorees/view/2008/5/ (accessed August 14, 2009).

Chapter 6

THE MONTGOMERY
BUS BOYCOTT

Montgomery, Alabama, 1955. An African American woman boards
a bus and sits in the colored section as required by the city segregation ordinance. The bus fills with passengers; they occupy all 35 seats.
When additional white passengers board the bus, the driver demands
that the black woman give up her seat so a white passenger may sit.
Tired of bus drivers pushing black passengers around, she refuses. After
repeated warnings, the bus driver calls the police and they arrest the
woman for violating city segregation ordinances. Who is she? Rosa
Parks? This incident could describe what happened when Rosa Parks
defied bus driver James F. Blake on December 1, 1955, but it could also
be the story of a number of brave, mostly forgotten African America
women in Montgomery who refused to give up their bus seats to white
patrons months before Rosa Parks's actions on December 1, 1955. And,
in fact, it is the story of four such women arrested by police before Rosa
Parks. Aurelia Browder, Susie McDonald, Claudette Colvin, and Mary
Louise Smith are not names well known in history, yet it was these four
women who served as plaintiffs in *Browder v. Gayle*, the U.S. District
Court case that eventually struck down segregation on Montgomery's
city bus system.[1]

Rosa Parks was fined $10 plus court costs for violating Mont-
gomery's segregation ordinance for city buses. On December 5,
1955, she posted bond for an appeal to the circuit court. The
bond was signed by E. D. Nixon (center) and Fred Gray,
one of Parks's attorneys. (AP Photo)

Claudette Colvin has become perhaps the best known of the plaintiffs. Police arrested Colvin in March 1955 when she refused to give up
her seat to a white man. As the police handcuffed, arrested, and forcibly removed her from the bus, Colvin screamed that the law violated
her constitutional rights. E. D. Nixon, president of the Montgomery
NAACP, and other activists were initially excited about organizing a
boycott around Colvin's case. They quickly lost interest, however, when
Nixon discovered that Colvin was several months pregnant. Nixon
and local attorney Fred Gray were uneasy about asking conservative-
minded African American churches to fight on behalf of Colvin, who
was also prone to outbursts and cursing. The court dropped many of the
charges against Colvin but a boycott and legal case never materialized
(see chapter 5). Then in April 1955, Aurelia Shines Browder, a graduate of Alabama State College, member of the Alpha Kappa Mu Honor

Society and the NAACP, who worked as a seamstress refused to give up her seat on the city bus to a white rider—seven months before Rosa Parks's historic arrest. Police took Browder to jail, the court fined her, and Browder filed a lawsuit against the city and Mayor W. A. "Tacky" Gayle. In February 1956, two months after the bus boycott sparked by Rosa Parks's arrest began, attorneys Fred Gray and Clifford Durr began searching for an ideal case to constitutionally challenge Alabama's city and state bus segregation laws, and they believed Mrs. Parks's case would not move beyond the state level. Gray approached Browder, Colvin, McDonald, and Smith, who all agreed to become plaintiffs in a civil action; Gray then filed *Browder v. Gayle* in U.S. District Court. The specific legal question before the court was whether the segregation on so-called privately owned buses operated by the City of Montgomery violated the 14th Amendment of the U.S. Constitution. Gray, who argued the case, said he chose Browder as the lead plaintiff "because she was a mature person, and I thought she would make an excellent first witness if I needed to put someone on [the witness stand]."[2] A three-judge panel decided *Browder v. Gayle* for the plaintiffs on June 4, 1956. The U.S. Supreme Court upheld the decision on November 13, 1956.[3] Rosa Parks's arrest is a far more prominent part of American history—it brought the indignities endured by African Americans to the public stage—but it was *Browder v. Gayle* and the four women who agreed to become plaintiffs that changed the *laws* applying to bus segregation in Montgomery.

So it was not Rosa Parks alone who brought about change in Montgomery. This important correction to the historical record about the events that took place in Montgomery in 1955 and 1956, however, does not diminish Parks's contribution to the struggle for black equality in America. Her arrest was the match that ignited the fire. The question is why—and the answer is partly because America was changing. Desegregation of the military, President Truman's Civil Rights Commission, *Brown v. Board of Education*, and increasing levels of organization among African Americans all played a part. Montgomery's African American community had already organized politically. Leaders such as E. D. Nixon, Mary Fair Burks, and JoAnn Robinson had brought the issues important to the black community to the mayor and city commissioners and taught African Americans to register and vote. Nor was Rosa

Parks the simply traditional, submissive African American laborer she seemed to be. Her secret activist life—secretary of the local NAACP, youth council advisor, and Highlander Folk School participant—gave her the will power and courage to fight against injustice. A young, articulate minister who was fairly new to Montgomery influenced Rosa Parks as well. In August, Dr. Martin Luther King, Jr., addressed about thirty people, most of them women, at the Metropolitan United Methodist Church on the *Brown v. Board of Education* decision. According to historian Douglas Brinkley, Rosa Parks and Johnnie Mae Carr sat mesmerized in the front of the church. Both women were greatly impressed with King's eloquence, his command of his subject, and his deep voice. Rosa Parks said of King, "I thought he was well prepared to take a role of leadership in the community."[4] A few days later, Rosa Parks wrote to King, inviting him to join the executive committee of the NAACP. A previous engagement kept King from attending the meeting, but Rosa Parks and King would work together soon enough.

Another event that hastened Rosa Parks's transition from a behind-the-scenes activist to a very public figure was the acquittal of two white men accused of the brutal lynching of Emmett Till. On August 13, 1955, Emmett Till, a 14-year-old from Chicago who was visiting family in Mississippi, was viciously murdered after he allegedly said, "Bye, baby" to Carolyn Bryant, a white woman storekeeper in Money, Mississippi. That night, Roy Bryant, Carolyn's husband, and his brother-in-law, J. W. Milam, abducted Till and murdered him. In addition to crushing his skull, gouging out one of his eyes, and shooting him in the head, they barb-wired a 75-pound cotton gin fan to his neck and threw is badly mutilated body into the Tallahatchie River. Emmett Till's murder appalled the nation and the world. Till's mother, Mamie Bradley, insisted on an open-casket funeral service for her son in Chicago. She wanted, she said, "The whole world to see" what racial hatred had done to her only child. National and international reporters covered the story, bringing worldwide criticism of Mississippi's segregationist society. *Jet* magazine published the grisly photo of Till's recovered body, his face so disfigured and distorted that readers, including Rosa Parks, became physically ill. Mamie Bradley's actions made her son's name a rallying cry in black America. The cry for justice became even stronger when, on September 23, 1955, after a five-day trial and deliberating for only 67 minutes, an all-white jury in Sumner, Mississippi, found Bryant and Milam not guilty.[5] Owing to the double jeopardy clause of the U.S. Constitution, Bryant and Milam could never be tried for Till's murder a second time. Several months later, Bryant and Milam bragged to William Bradford Huie, a journalist, that they had murdered Till, and Huie then published their story in *Look* magazine.[6]

According to Parks, she was well aware that the Montgomery NAACP was looking for a plaintiff who was beyond reproach to be a test case in the courts because she was in on those discussions. However, she clearly stated that this was not the reason she refused to give up her seat on the bus to a white man on December 1, 1955. Despite all speculation to the contrary, Rosa Parks was *not* an NAACP plant on the bus that day. She quite forcefully made this assertion throughout her life. Speaking at a tribute dinner in 1965, Parks said, "I spontaneously made that decision without any leadership. You can't be told what to do. You have to be motivated—you have to feel that you will not be pushed around."[7] And in her autobiography, Parks wrote that not only did she not intend to be arrested, but she would have avoided boarding the bus had she noticed who the driver was.[8] According to her childhood friend Johnnie Mae Carr, "She did not set out to do what actually happened.... Rosa was not thinking about what the aftermath would be."[9]

Parks had other things on her mind that Thursday evening. The Montgomery Fair department store made nearly half its sales between Thanksgiving and New Year's Day, so during the holiday season the tailor shop was extremely busy. Parks had to alter, hem, iron, or steampress dresses and suits in record time. More importantly, Parks was also busy with NAACP business. She was responsible for organizing the NAACP workshop scheduled for December 3 and 4 on the Alabama State College campus. She had spent a good deal of her break time trying to get H. Council Trenholm, president of the college, to approve the use of a building on Saturday morning. In addition, Parks had to get the notices for the election of NAACP Senior Branch officers the following week into the mail. She had lunch with Attorney Fred Gray and then returned to work.[10]

When she left work at 5:00 P.M., Parks went to Court Square to wait for her bus. However, when the Cleveland Avenue bus arrived, it was crowded, so Parks decided to do some shopping and catch a later bus. After buying a few items, Parks walked to the bus stop and waited. When the bus came, she boarded and paid her fare. As she later wrote, only after paying did she recognize the driver as the same "mean-looking" man who had put her off the bus 12 years earlier. If she had not been distracted, Parks would not have gotten on Blake's bus. In the years since the 1943 incident, she usually had managed to avoid doing so.[11]

After boarding the bus, Parks took the first open seat in the colored section of the bus. There was a man next to the window and two women across the aisle. There were only a few open seats in the white section. At the next stop, several whites boarded the bus and took the open seats. One white man remained standing. When the driver looked back and saw the white man standing, he said, "Let me have those front seats." Of course he meant the front seats in the colored section. No one moved. Then the driver told Parks and the three other passengers in the row, "Y'all better make it light on yourselves and let me have those seats." The man sitting in the window seat next to Parks stood and she moved to let him pass. The two women across the aisle stood to move as well. Parks moved to the window seat. In her autobiography, Parks wrote that at that moment she had reflected that complying with such demands had only increased the contempt with which blacks were treated. She remembered sitting up with her grandfather, his gun by the fireplace. Those who claimed that she had refused to yield her seat because she was tired were mistaken; at age 42, she was no more tired after work that day than she was on any other. Rather, "the only tired I was, was tired of giving in."[12] In a later interview, Parks remembered, "At this point I felt that, if I did stand up, it meant that I approved of the way I was being treated, and I did not approve."[13] James Blake, the driver, asked Parks if she was going to get up and she said no. He told her that if she did not move, he would call the police and have her arrested. She looked at him and said simply, "You may do that." Blake left the bus to wait for the police to arrive. As Parks sat on the bus, she contemplated what might happen next. She knew the police would arrest her, but she knew that they might push her around or beat her as well. Parks wrote that she tried not to think about the possibilities because if she thought too hard, she might have gotten off the bus. Nevertheless, she chose to remain.[14] In an interview in 1991, Parks recalled,

> I wasn't scared or frightened but I was determined to let them know I was not happy with the way I was being treated. Under segregation, you had to put aside your dignity. . . . It was very unpleasant. It made you feel like you were not being treated like a human being.[15]

Two police officers arrived; one asked Parks why she refused to stand up. She looked up at him and simply asked, "Why do you all push us around?" He replied, "I don't know, but the law is the law and you're under arrest." The officers picked up her personal belongings and took her to the police car. They did not touch her or force her into the police car. The police asked Blake if he wanted to swear out a warrant for Parks's arrest. He said he would come to the station when he finished his route. Parks remained in custody although not yet under arrest until Blake arrived at the station. After the police officers completed their paperwork, Parks asked to make a phone call. The officers said no. They took her to the city jail, where they went through the booking process, confiscating her personal belongings, fingerprinting her, and taking her mug shot. A white matron then took Parks to her jail cell. A short time later, the matron returned and led Parks to the telephone, from which she called home. After determining that the police had not beaten her, Raymond told Rosa that he would come there to get her out. By the time Rosa Parks called home, word was already out about her arrest. A family friend came by Parks's apartment just as she was speaking to Raymond and offered to drive him to the jail. Bertha Butler, who had seen Parks taken off the bus, was E. D. Nixon's neighbor; she told the Nixons of Parks's arrest. Word spread like wildfire throughout the community—the police had arrested Rosa Parks for refusing to give up her seat on the bus. Nixon called Fred Gray, one of the two African American attorneys in Montgomery, but Gray was away, so he called Clifford Durr. Durr called the jail, asking what the charges were and the amount needed for bail. Because of Parks's arrest, Clifford Durr became the first white attorney in the civil rights movement.[16] Parks spent very little time in jail. Raymond Parks, Nixon, and Durr rushed to pay her bail and have her released.[17]

Virginia Durr was with the men when they arrived at the jail. According to Durr,

> Everything went very smoothly. They brought Mrs. Parks out
> from behind the bars. That was a terrible sight to me to see this
> gentle, lovely, sweet woman, whom I knew and was so fond of,
> being brought down by a matron. She wasn't in handcuffs, but
> they had to unlock two or three doors that grated loudly. She was
> very calm.[18]

Clifford Durr and E. D. Nixon went to the desk with Parks, where she gathered her personal belongings. The trial date was set for Monday, December 5, 1955. Parks recalled later that few words were exchanged, yet only when she was released did she realize just how much her stint in jail had upset her.[19]

After Rosa's release, she and Raymond, the Durrs, and Nixon went to the Parks's small apartment on Cleveland Avenue. There, along with Rosa Parks's mother, Leona, the group discussed the case. Nixon thought Parks's case could be the test case for which the NAACP had been searching. According to Nixon, "Rosa Parks was just the right person at the right time."[20] Nixon saw Rosa Parks as the perfect plaintiff. He recalled,

> Rosa Parks worked with me for twelve years prior to this. She was
> secretary for everything I had going—the Brotherhood of Sleep-
> ing Car Porters, NAACP, Alabama Voters' League, all of those
> things....She was honest, she was clean, and she had integrity.
> The press couldn't go out and dig up something she did last year,
> or last month, or five years ago. They couldn't hang nothing like
> that on Rosa Parks.[21]

Despite Nixon's excitement at the prospect of a test case with the perfect plaintiff, he had to convince the Parkses. Raymond Parks was very reluctant. According to Virginia Durr, he repeatedly told Rosa, "the white folks will kill you."[22] And, in fact, this was a monumental decision for the family. Rosa was the family's main breadwinner. If she decided to go along with Nixon, she was certain to lose her job.

More importantly, she would become a very public figure; Raymond and her mother were certain a mob would lynch her. Even if this did not happen, Rosa knew that whites might target Raymond—the police might harass him or arrest him on false charges. Her mother's health was not good—could Leona withstand the stress? Clifford Durr asked Parks if she wanted to test the constitutionality of the segregation law or if she wanted him to try to have the charges dropped to prevent a long court trial. Raymond, Leona, and Rosa discussed and debated the issues, and according to Rosa Parks,

> In the end [Raymond] Parks and my mother supported the idea. They were against segregation and were willing to fight it. And I had worked on enough cases to know that a ruling could not be made without a plaintiff. So I agreed to be the plaintiff.[23]

Both Clifford Durr and Fred Gray decided the case had to be supported by the NAACP Legal Defense Fund—since the case would have to go all the way to the U.S. Supreme Court.[24]

About 11:30 P.M., Gray, who had returned to Montgomery after being out of town most of the day, called JoAnn Robinson of the Women's Political Council (WPC). The WPC had been preparing for a test case; they were ready to distribute thousands of notices asking African Americans to stay off the buses on Monday, December 5, 1955, the day of Rosa Parks's trial. Robinson sat down and wrote the notice.

> Another Negro woman has been arrested and thrown in jail because she refused to get up out of her seat on the bus for a white person to sit down. It is the second time since the Claudette Colvin case that a Negro woman has been arrested for the same thing. This has to be stopped. Negroes have rights, too, for if Negroes did not ride the buses, they could not operate. Three-fourths of the riders are Negroes, yet we are arrested, or have to stand over empty seats. If we do not do something to stop these arrests, they will continue. The next time it may be you, or your daughter, or your mother. This woman's case will come up on Monday. We are, therefore, asking every Negro to stay off the buses Monday in protest of the arrest and trial. Don't ride the buses to work, to town,

to school, or anywhere on Monday. You can afford to stay out of
school for one day if you have no other way to go except by bus.
You can also afford to stay out of town for one day. If you work,
take a cab, or walk. But please, children and grown-ups, don't ride
the bus at all on Monday. Please stay off of all buses on Monday.[25]

By 4 A.M., Robinson, two of her most trusted students, and John Can-
non, chairman of the business department at Alabama State College, had
mimeographed the notice. Between 4 and 7 A.M., Robinson and her students mapped out distribution routes for the notices, arranged the bundles,
and stacked them in their cars. After Robinson's 8 A.M. class, she contacted other members of the WPC and other activists to help distributing
the leaflets. Robinson and the students dropped off tens of thousands of
notices to schools, businesses, beauty shops, saloons, factories, and bar-
bershops. The people in these places passed them on to other employees
and customers. Robinson recalled that the whole action proceeded so
smoothly that the city and its residents never suspected a thing. By 2 P.M.,
distribution was complete, and according to Robinson, "Practically every
black man, woman, and child in Montgomery knew the plan and was
passing the word along. No one knew where the notices had come from
or who had arranged for their circulation, and no one cared."[26] And so far,
Montgomery's white community knew nothing about the plans.

Of course, the organizers could not know whether African Americans would stay off the buses on Monday. They were not even sure if
the entire black community knew about the plans. What they did learn
by Friday afternoon was that someone had let the white community
know what was up. The *Alabama Journal* ran a story about the planned
boycott on Saturday afternoon. On Sunday, an article appeared in the
Montgomery Advertiser; the news was also broadcast by two local television stations and all four-radio stations. According to Robinson, the
organizers hoped to keep the boycott a complete secret and surprise
whites, but in retrospect "One good thing, however, came from the revelation: the few black citizens in remote corners of the city who might
not have gotten the news of the boycott, knew it now."[27]

Black leaders and ministers met on Friday night at Dexter Avenue
Baptist Church to set up committees on transportation, map out routes,
and create a pickup system for black workers. According to Virginia

Durr, E. D. Nixon made an emotional plea to the crowd: "I'm a Pull-man porter and every time I go on my job, I put on an apron or a jacket. You know, we've been wearing aprons for three hundred years. It's time we took off our aprons."[28] The one hundred leaders attending the meeting formed the Montgomery Improvement Association (MIA), elected Martin Luther, King, Jr., president, and called for a mass meeting at Holt Street Baptist Church on Monday evening following the one-day boycott. The goals of the Monday evening meeting, according to Robinson, was to calm emotions, prevent violence between blacks and whites, and get a clear report on the effectiveness of the boycott. The question on everyone's mind was: Should the boycott continue? The WPC prepared flyers about the Monday evening meeting and circulated them throughout the city.[29]

Meanwhile, on Friday morning, Rosa Parks called a taxi to take her to work. John Ball, who was in charge of men's alterations, was shocked when Parks walked into Montgomery Fair. Ball believed Parks would "be a nervous wreck." During lunch, Parks went to Fred Gray's office, which was "like a beehive" of activity because of the boycott. After work, Parks went to the meeting at the Dexter Avenue Baptist Church to tell the leaders exactly what had happened the previous day. All the ministers who stayed for the entire meeting agreed to tell their congregations about the protest during their Sunday sermons.[30]

On Monday morning the bus drivers rolled out the Montgomery City Lines buses and began their routes, each one with two motorcycle policemen trailing the buses to "protect Negro riders" who would want to ride the bus from violence by the boycotters. Newspaper articles that morning reported that boycotters had formed "Negro goon squads" to intimidate law-abiding black riders. The motorcycle police were "to maintain law and order." The black community ignored or scoffed at the reports, and no passengers waited for the buses. Hundreds of African Americans were walking, boarding taxis, or using private cars. The buses remained empty throughout the day; even whites stayed off them.[31]

Rosa Parks did not go to work on Monday. Instead, she headed to the courthouse for her trial, accompanied by her husband and E. D. Nixon. People packed the courthouse and the street that day; police almost did not let Raymond in until he explained he was Rosa's husband. The crowd was chanting and shouting its support for Rosa Parks. One

Martin Luther King, Jr., delivered an impassioned address at a mass meeting at the Holt Street Baptist Church on January 1, 1956, less than a month after the Montgomery Improvement Association met there and committed themselves to continuing the Montgomery bus boycott. (AP Photo/Gene Herrick)

young woman said, "Oh, she's so sweet. They've messed with the wrong one now." The trial itself was short. The bus driver, James F. Blake, was the main witness for the prosecution. A white woman testified that there was an open seat in the back of the bus and Parks refused to take it—a blatant lie. Rosa Parks did not testify in her own behalf. Parks's attorneys, Fred Gray and Charles Langford, entered a not guilty plea for her. For Parks's court case to become a test case, the court would have to find her guilty, as she and her attorneys understood. Her attorneys would then appeal the conviction to a higher court. The judge quickly ruled that Rosa Parks was guilty of violating the segregation laws and then fined her $10 plus $4 in court costs.[32] Rosa Parks left the courthouse and went to Fred Gray's office, where she answered the phone and took messages until Nixon took her home to get ready for the Holt Street Baptist Church meeting that evening.[33]

On Friday night, the ministers had selected Martin Luther King, Jr., to be the speaker on Monday evening and had also chosen him to be the president of the MIA. According to E. D. Nixon, the group chose King because he was new to Montgomery and had not had enough time to make any strong friends or enemies. King electrified the crowd of ten to fifteen thousand African Americans in and around the church.

> And you know, my friends, there comes a time when people get tired of being trampled over by the iron feet of oppression. There comes a time, my friends, when people get tired of being plunged across the abyss of humiliation where they experience the bleakness of nagging despair.... There comes a time....
>
> We are here, we are here this evening because we're tired now. And I want to say, that we are not here advocating violence. We have never done that. I want it to be known throughout Montgomery and throughout this nation that we are Christian people. We believe in the Christian religion. We believe in the teachings of Jesus. The only weapon that we have in our hands this evening is the weapon of protest.
>
> And we are not wrong, we are not wrong in what we are doing. If we are wrong, the Supreme Court of this nation is wrong. If we are wrong, the Constitution of the United States is wrong. If we are wrong, God Almighty is wrong. If we are wrong, Jesus of Nazareth was merely a utopian dreamer that never came down to earth. If we are wrong, justice is a lie: love has no meaning. And we are determined here in Montgomery to work and fight until justice runs down like water and righteousness like a mighty stream.[34]

King's speech was spellbinding; it struck just the right balance. The speech was militant enough to keep the people aroused and willing to go on and yet moderate enough to keep their passions within controllable and "Christian" limits. King said,

> I knew that many of the Negro people were victims of bitterness that could easily rise to flood proportions. What could I say to keep them courageous and prepared for positive action and yet devoid of hate and resentment? Could the militant and the moderate be combined in a single speech?[35]

The answer was a resounding yes.

After King's speech, Reverend E. N. French introduced Rosa Parks, and Reverend Ralph Abernathy read a three-page resolution asking that all African Americans—and fair-minded whites—stay off the buses until the MIA could negotiate a settlement with city officials. The vote was unanimous—the boycott would continue.[36] On December 8, MIA members met with the city commissioners and bus company representatives. The MIA leaders announced the three conditions that they wanted met before the boycott would end. First, they wanted courteous treatment of black passengers. Second, black passengers would sit from the rear toward the front and whites from the front toward the rear until passengers filled all the seats—no one would surrender a seat, no one would have to stand over an empty seat. Third, the bus company would employ black drivers on predominately black routes. King pointed out that African Americans were not demanding changes in the segregation laws; rather, they wanted better treatment and justice for black passengers. After five hours, the meeting ended at an impasse; no further meeting was scheduled and nothing changed.[37] It was clear that the boycott would continue, but no one would have thought that African Americans in Montgomery would continue the boycott for 381 days.

Everyone involved in the boycott knew the risks they were taking, but they could not always envision the form those risks would take. White sympathizers found themselves ostracized, received threatening phone calls, or lost their friends and jobs. In a letter to the editor of the *Montgomery Advertiser*, librarian Juliette Morgan wrote of her respect for African Americans and her support for their cause. Immediately after her letter appeared, she began to receive threatening phone calls, many of her friends deserted her, and she lost her job. About a year after the letter appeared, Morgan failed to answer her phone. Close friends went to her home to check on her; they found that she had taken her own life. After a newspaper article detailing the support given to the boycott by Reverend Robert Graetz, a white minister of a black congregation, the Graetz family began getting threatening phone calls, intruders vandalized their home, and prowlers made verbal threats that were heard a block away. In August, someone bombed Graetz's home, and later his home was bombed again. Many in the white community targeted Clifford and Virginia Durr, publicly scorning and socially ostracizing them.[38] White supporters were a small and threatened group indeed.

Some whites, staunch supporters of segregation, decided to organize, forming the White Citizens Council (WCC) to preserve segregation at all costs. The Montgomery WCC was a small albeit vigilant group. On December 22, the WCC decided to take action through a paid political advertisement, "Wake Up and Ride the Bus." The ad implied that the bus boycott was over, but blacks saw through the ruse. Then, on December 30, the WCC announced that it would give a "$100 reward for the apprehension of parties guilty of violence to city buses," and then tried to entice city leaders into joining the group to "put black people, once and for all, where they belonged." Advertisements appeared in the newspapers daily for whites to, "JOIN THE WHITE CITIZENS COUNCIL...Help to preserve segregation in Alabama." Virginia Durr reported that, "the White Citizens Councils grow apace day by day and there is real blackmail going on. They work the blocks and buildings and ask each one to join and if they don't—Well, there is no doubt you get on a blacklist." One liberal white man told Durr that he was leaving town because "if he didn't join the WCC he simply could not make a living here at all."[39] By January 1956, WCC membership had expanded. In Montgomery, Clyde Sellers, the city police commissioner, publicly joined the group.[40]

Meanwhile, the MIA organized a transportation committee and created a carpool system with specific dropoff and pickup locations for the former black bus passengers. African Americans who owned cars worked in specific areas driving the passengers to wherever they had to go without charge. At first people used their cars and paid for their own gas, but as the boycott wore on, churches began taking up collections to pay for gas. However, when news of the boycott spread throughout the country, money began to come in from everywhere. In New York, Bayard Rustin, a black activist, Stanley Levinson, and Ella Baker formed In Friendship, which held rallies to raise money supporting civil rights actions in the South. In May 1956, the group sent $2,000 to the MIA for the boycott. In addition, Baker spent many weeks in Montgomery attending meetings each night and discussing the direction in which the civil rights movement should move. Baker helped wherever she could in Montgomery, working closely with E. D. Nixon and

Virginia Durr to further the boycott. Baker, who had met Rosa Parks at an NAACP leadership meeting in 1946, now reunited with Parks and conducted a fund-raising tour throughout the Northeast to raise the funds needed to keep the carpool going.[41]

By the end of January, Sellers instructed the police to disburse groups of blacks who were loitering in white residential areas. Of course, these "loiterers" were maids, cooks, and nurses waiting for rides at the pickup stations blacks had set up to transport people to work. Police began ticketing black drivers for speeding, failing to stop at red lights, failing to slow down at a yield sign, staying too long at stop signs, or not staying long enough. JoAnn Robinson received 17 tickets for all types of phony charges. Police arrested and jailed King for alleg-edly driving 30 miles an hour in a 25-mile zone, and black cab drivers found themselves in jail for not displaying the proper legal papers in their windows. White teenagers drove through black neighborhoods harassing walkers and shouting, "Walk, nigger, walk" or throwing water on black pedestrians. Eventually the teenagers replaced the water with urine, rotten eggs, potatoes, or bricks. The WCC burned crosses. Then, on January 30, 1956, things became more violent. An unknown person or persons threw a bomb on King's front porch while he was away attending a meeting. The explosion shattered the glass in the front window, split a section of the porch, and made a hole in the porch floor. King's wife, Coretta, and his daughter, Yolanda, were at home, but neither was injured. Although the city commission offered a $500 reward for the "capture and conviction of the guilty ones," police never apprehended the person or persons responsible for the attack. Then, on February 1, someone bombed E. D. Nixon's home. Nixon, who was off working at his porter's job, was not home at the time, and the bombing did not receive nearly as much attention as the King bombing.[42]

In February 21, 1956, a Montgomery Grand Jury indicted 89 bus boycott leaders, including King and Parks and most of the other black ministers, for violating a 1921 state statute that barred boycotts with-out "just cause." On February 22, 75 of the indicted boycott leaders appeared at the county jail, where they were arrested and released on bond. The New York Times printed a photograph of police fingerprint-ing Rosa Parks, and later people chronicling the boycott would identify

Rosa Parks, charged with violating city segregation laws, is fingerprinted by police lieutenant D. H. Lackey in Montgomery on February 22, 1956. (AP Photo/Gene Herrick)

the photo as coming from Parks's first arrest. Of the 89 people indicted, only King went to trial. The court found him guilty and fined him $500 and one year at hard labor. The Appeals Court overturned the decision. In addition to all of this, Judge Eugene Carter upheld Rosa Parks's conviction, and the Montgomery City Attorney moved to dismiss the suit filed by Gray and Langford in federal district court. According to Rosa Parks, the white legal establishment did everything within its power to stop the boycott.[43]

It was a time of increasing hardship for the Parkses as well. Rosa Parks became a board member of the MIA and participated in not only the bus boycott but also the boycotting of white-owned stores that December. She donated the money she saved to the MIA transportation fund that paid for cars, gasoline, and insurance for volunteer drivers. Raymond Parks resigned his position as a barber at Maxwell Field Air Force Base because his supervisor ordered that there was to be no discussion of "the bus protest or Rosa Parks in his establishment." Raymond Parks refused to work in a place where he could not mention his wife's name. Then, on January 7, 1956, the Montgomery Fair department store discharged Rosa Parks. The personnel officer did not say it was because of the boycott; rather, he told her it was because their tailor was leaving and starting his own shop. If the store had no tailor, there was no need for a tailor's assistant. Montgomery Fair closed its tailor shop, giving Rosa two weeks' pay and her bonus money. Then the Parkses' landlord raised the rent on their small apartment. Rosa recalled that after her dismissal she took in sewing at home to make ends meet, did work for the MIA, and traveled, making appearances because of her arrest and the boycott. As an MIA board member, she dispensed clothing and shoes to people who needed them and worked as a dispatcher for the MIA's transportation committee. According to Virginia Durr, in the spring of 1956, Parks traveled to Seattle, Oakland and San Francisco, and New York City to speak on behalf of the NAACP. Myles Horton invited Parks to return to Highlander in the December of 1956, not as a student but as a speaker. Parks, her mother, and Nixon traveled to Highlander, where Rosa spoke to six black students who were trying to integrate the schools in Clinton, Tennessee. According to Parks, the staff at Highlander asked her to live and work at Highlander, as Septima Clark did, but Leona objected. Parks did return to Highlander for additional workshops, and attended Highlander's 25th anniversary with King.[44]

Virginia Durr did her best to help the Parkses as well. In February 1956, Durr wrote to her friend Jessica "Decca" Mitford, asking that she try to raise money to send to Rosa. "She has lost her job and is having a very hard time ... She is the main figure in the boycott and her case will come up soon and she has to stay here and is having a hard time getting work," Durr wrote. "Do try and raise some money for Mrs. Parks who has the heaviest burden to bear and is wonderful, really wonderful, and so brave and good. They also raised her rent."[45] In late February, Durr again wrote to Mitford reporting, "I saw Mrs. Parks yesterday and she has gotten enough money for herself to relieve her own personal difficulties." According to Durr, "Mrs. Parks got over $500 from the various letters I wrote." Parks suggested to Durr that fundraising efforts should now focus on helping the "Protest (they are not calling it a Boycott

Raymond Parks accompanied his wife to the circuit court for her arraignment, February 24, 1956. (AP Photo)

any more since they were all indicted for boycotting)."[46] The protest continued until the U.S. Supreme Court issued its *Browder v. Gayle* decision—which said that Montgomery's buses had to be integrated. On December 20, 1956, U.S. marshals formally served the Court's orders on Montgomery's city officials. The next morning, Montgomery City Lines resumed full service. Dr. King, the Reverend Ralph Abernathy, E. D. Nixon, and Glen Smiley, a white boycott supporter, boarded a bus and sat in seats previously reserved for whites, while *Look* magazine snapped photographs. In her memoirs, JoAnn Robinson wrote that Rosa Parks was there as well, but Parks disputed that. Parks remembered that she planned to stay home to care for her sick mother when three reporters from *Look* magazine came to her apartment and asked her to come downtown so that they could take pictures of her getting on and off the bus. Parks reported that James Blake was the driver on one of the buses she boarded.[47]

The Montgomery Bus Boycott was over, but not the trouble. "Snipers shot at buses . . . a group tried to start a whites-only bus service . . . the homes of two black leaders, four Baptists churches, the People's Service Station and Cab Stand, and the home of another black were all

The success of the bus boycott provoked a fierce
backlash among segregationist whites. Here, robed
Klansmen walk to a cross-burning rally held in
Montgomery on November 24, 1956. The end of
the boycott less than a month later did not end racist
violence. (AP Photo)

bombed." In addition, someone placed a bomb on King's front porch, but it did not explode. Police arrested seven white men for the bombings, and the grand jury indicted five. A jury found two defendants, Raymond D. York and Sonny Kyle Livingston, not guilty, even though they had signed confessions. The rest of the accused men were set free under a compromise that also canceled the cases of blacks arrested under the antiboycott laws.[48]

Nevertheless, black residents of Montgomery could now ride city buses as equals, and thanks to their efforts, many other black citizens throughout the nation—in Birmingham, Alabama, and Tallahassee, Florida—started boycotts against segregated buses in their cities. The events in Montgomery catapulted Martin Luther King, Jr., to national recognition. From this point on, white America would recognize King as the spokesman for black Americans. In addition, King would organize a new civil rights organization—the Southern Christian Leadership Conference (SCLC), which would become the most visible civil rights organization of the 1960s.

Others who helped initiate and lead the boycott were not so fortunate. Between 1958 and 1960, a special state committee investigated teachers at Alabama State College who had supported the boycott. Because of that investigation, white state evaluators began visiting classes, creating a strain on the administration, faculty, and students. The evaluators meant to create an atmosphere of intimidation, and they succeeded. Their presence wore down many teachers, including Mary Fair Burks and JoAnn Robinson. In 1960, a considerable number of teachers, including Burks and Robinson, chose to resign their teaching positions.[49]

E. D. Nixon left the Montgomery Improvement Association after a dispute with some of MIA's leaders over class-based divisions within the organization; He was also displeased with King for turning the MIA into "a one-man show" and using Rosa Parks for its own purposes and then abandoning her.[50] In a letter to Clark Foreman, Virginia Durr said, "There is a blazing row going on down here" between King and Nixon.[51] Nixon continued to be an activist for the black community in voter registration and fair housing, although in a less visible way, and worked as the recreation director of a public housing project. By the late 1960s, Nixon had lost much of his political influence and faded into the background. The media focused its attention on King, ignoring the major contributions of Nixon and others. Nixon died on February 25, 1987, at Baptist Hospital in Montgomery. In 2001, the Montgomery County Public School System named an elementary school for him in recognition of his contributions to the civil rights movement.[52]

The boycott generated a mixed legacy for Rosa Parks. The media gave her a great deal of attention during the boycott, of course, and being a public figure brought with it many complications. Almost instantly, Parks became the most famous African American woman in America. Black communities everywhere celebrated her, but among her colleagues, jealousy and male chauvinism held center court. According to historian Douglas Brinkley, one Baptist minister said to Parks, "Well! If it isn't the superstar!" Even E. D. Nixon, the man Parks strongly supported through her work with him in the NAACP and the

Brotherhood of Sleeping Car Porters, began to resent the attention she was receiving. Brinkley writes that Nixon told Daisy Bates, an Arkansas NAACP activist, that Parks was a "lovely, stupid woman." The other women who were instrumental to the boycott resented Parks as well. Aurelia Browder, the lead plaintiff in the *Browder* case, believed she deserved public recognition too. Claudette Colvin said she was "angry that everybody was saying 'Rosa this' and 'Rosa that'" and that she "felt ostracized by the black community."[53]

By the end of the boycott, Rosa Parks was overwhelmed by these attitudes as well as by money problems; she also had to deal with her fragile, ill mother, and a husband who had suffered a nervous breakdown because of the constant harassment the family endured during and after the boycott. The MIA refused to hire Rosa for one if its paid positions. Virginia Durr wrote that Rosa Parks had "been a heroine everywhere else, [but] they have not given her a job although she has needed one desperately."[54] Parks was on edge. But no matter how much King and the other ministers neglected her, they could not deny that it had been Rosa Parks who had ignited the event that initiated a new phase of the civil rights movement. The nonviolent, direct-action stage of the movement had begun, and it would have historic consequences.

NOTES

1. Tim Walker, *Browder v. Gayle*: "The Women Before Rosa Parks," http://www.tolerance.org/teach/activities/activity.jsp?cid=388 (accessed August 17, 2009); Jannell McGrew, "Aurelia Shines Browder Coleman," *Montgomery Advertiser*, http://www.montgomeryboycott.com/profile_browder.htm (accessed August 17, 2009).

2. McGrew, "Aurelia Shines Browder Coleman."

3. "Teaching With Documents: An Act of Courage, The Arrest Records of Rosa Parks," The National Archives, http://www.archives.gov/education/lessons/rosa-parks/ (accessed August 17, 2009).

4. Douglas Brinkley, *Rosa Parks; A Life* (New York: Penguin Books, 2000), 100; Rosa Parks with Jim Haskins, *My Story* (New York: Penguin Books, 1992), 139.

5. Stephen J. Whitfield, *A Death in the Delta: The Story of Emmett Till* (Baltimore: Johns Hopkins University Press, 1991).

6. Richard Rubin, "The Ghosts of Emmett Till," *New York Times Magazine* (July 31, 2005).

7. Rosa L. Parks Papers, Walter Reuther Archives of Labor and Urban Affairs, Wayne State University, box 1, folder 2.

8. Parks, *My Story*, 113.

9. Jannell McGrew, "Close Friend, Activist Has Special Perspective," *Montgomery Advertiser* (April 6, 2009), http://www.montgomeryadver tiser.com/apps/pbcs.dll/article?AID=/99999999/NEWS/61113023/1001 (accessed August 21, 2009).

10. Parks, *My Story*, 112–13; Brinkley, *Rosa Parks*, 104–5.

11. Parks, *My Story*, 113.

12. Rosa Parks interview, Sound Roll 1525, Camera Roll 557, http:// www.teachersdomain.org/resource/iml04.soc.ush.civil.parks/ Tran script, 3 (accessed August 18, 2009); Parks, *My Story*, 115–16.

13. Marcia M. Greenlee, "Interview with Rosa McCauley Parks" on August 22 and 23, 1978, in *The Black Woman Oral History Project*, vol. 8, ed. Ruth Edmonds Hill (Westport, CT: Meckler, 1991), 248.

14. Parks, *My Story*, 116.

15. John Mitchell, "Bus Ride that Moves a Nation is Recalled," *Los Angeles Times*, January 25, 1991, Metro Section, 1.

16. Sarah Hart Brown, *Standing Against Dragons: Three Southern Lawyers in a Era of Fear* (Baton Rouge: Louisiana State University Press, 1998), 148.

17. Manning Marable, *Let Nobody Turn Us Around* (New York: Rowman and Littlefield, 2009), 354; Parks, *My Story*, 117–22.

18. Virginia Durr, *Outside the Magic Circle: The Autobiography of Virginia Foster Durr*, ed. Hollinger F. Barnard (Birmingham: University of Alabama Press, 1985), 280.

19. Parks, *My Story*, 123.

20. Al Martinez, "'Mother of Civil Rights' a Reluctant Celebrity," *Los Angeles Times*, September 13, 1980, A1.

21. Parks, *My Story*, 125.

22. Durr, *Outside the Magic Circle*, 280.

23. Parks, *My Story*, 124; Durr, *Outside the Magic Circle*, 280–81.

24. Durr, *Outside the Magic Circle*, 281.

25. JoAnn Robinson, *The Montgomery Bus Boycott and the Women Who Started It* (Knoxville: University of Tennessee Press, 1987) 46.

26. Ibid., 46–47.

27. Ibid., 55.

28. Durr, *Outside the Magic Circle*, 281.

29. Robinson, *The Montgomery Bus Boycott and the Women Who Started It*, 56.

30. Parks, *My Story*, 128–29.

31. Ibid., 130–32; Robinson, *The Montgomery Bus Boycott and the Women Who Started It*, 57–59.

32. Parks, *My Story*, 133–34.

33. Ibid., 134.

34. Martin Luther King, Jr., Papers, MIA Mass Meeting at Holt Street Baptist Church, December 5, 1955, Montgomery, AL, http://www.stanford.edu/group/King/papers/vol3/551205.004-MIA_Mass_Meeting_at_Holt_Street_Baptist_Church.htm (accessed August 18, 2009).

35. Ibid.

36. Wayne Phillips, "Negroes Pledge to Keep Boycott," *New York Times* (February 24, 1956); Parks, *My Story*, 140; Brinkley, *Rosa Parks*, 140.

37. Levi Watkins Learning Center, Alabama State University, Montgomery Improvement Association Papers, box 1, folder 3; Robinson, *The Montgomery Bus Boycott and the Women Who Started It*, 78–81.

38. Robinson, *The Montgomery Bus Boycott and the Women Who Started It*, 102–4.

39. Patricia Sullivan, ed., *Freedom Writer: Virginia Foster Durr, Letters from the Civil Rights Years* (New York: Routledge, 2003), 109.

40. Robinson, *The Montgomery Bus Boycott and the Women Who Started It*, 111–2.

41. Joann Grant, *Ella Baker: Freedom Bound* (New York: Wiley, 1999), 101–2.

42. Robinson, *The Montgomery Bus Boycott and the Women Who Started It*, 124–33; Encyclopedia of Alabama, http://www.encyclopediaofalabama.org/face/Article.jsp?id=h-1355 (accessed August 19, 2009); Parks, *My Story*, 142.

43. Eugene W. Carter Papers, Alabama State Archives; Martin Luther King, Jr. Papers, http://mlk-kpp01.stanford.edu/index.php/king papers/article/volume_3_birth_of_a_new_age_chronology/ (accessed August 19, 2009); Rosa Parks, *My Story*, 142–150.

44. Sullivan, *Freedom Writer*, 110–22; Parks, *My Story*, 142–57.

45. Sullivan, *Freedom Writer*, 106–7.

46. Ibid., 110–12.

47. Robinson, *The Montgomery Bus Boycott and the Women Who Started It*, 162–63; Parks, *My Story*, 157–58.

48. The Montgomery Bus Boycott, http://www.watson.org/~lisa/black history/civilrights-55–65/montbus.html (accessed August 19, 2009).

49. Robinson, *The Montgomery Bus Boycott and the Women Who Started It*, 169.

50. Lynne Olson, *Freedom's Daughters: The Unsung Heroines of the Civil Rights Movement from 1830 to 1970* (New York: Simon and Schuster, 2001), 129.

51. Sullivan, *Freedom Writer*, 138.

52. "E. D. Nixon," Encyclopedia of Alabama, http://www.encyclo pediaofalabama.org/face/Article.jsp?id=h-1355 (accessed August 20, 2009).

53. Brinkley, *Rosa Parks*, 175.

54. Olson, *Freedom's Daughters*, 129.

Chapter 7

LIFE IN DETROIT

Rosa Parks did not stay in Montgomery long after the boycott ended. In August 1957, the family moved to Detroit, where her brother Sylvester had moved after World War II. Life in Montgomery had become dangerous; threatening phone calls came at all hours of the day and night. Parks recalled that Raymond began sleeping with a gun nearby, and her mother, Leona, would call a neighbor and talk for long periods just to tie up the phone lines so the hate calls could not get through. When Rosa went out, whites would recognize her and some made "hateful remark[s]." Death threats arrived in the mail as well. One person was particularly virulent in the attacks, telling Parks that she would burn in hell for the things she had done in Montgomery and threatening her with physical violence. With no jobs and no money for moving expenses, Parks turned to a cousin, Thomas Williamson, from Detroit for help. Williamson sent Parks $300 and the Parks family began packing.[1]

When Montgomery's African American community heard that Parks was leaving, they were shocked and ashamed over their recent comments and behavior toward her. The apologies and contrition came too late, but in a last-ditch attempt to salve their consciences, the MIA held a farewell testimonial for Parks and collected $800 as a going-away present. Virginia Durr spoke at the dinner, but it was Rosa's remarks that she remembered best. According to Durr, "She made the most wonderful speech that night, and told them that they could never win unless they fought for the right of everyone to have opportunities, and not just themselves." In her own understated way, Parks addressed the growing divisions within the MIA and Montgomery's black community. "I do miss her so much," Durr continued, "as she was such a fine and firm person, not exactly concrete but at least mighty firm asphalt. I feel now that I am paved with pebbles or cobblestones, firm but rough and shaky."[2]

In August 1957, the Parks family arrived in Detroit. Although Parks recalled that her brother, Sylvester McCauley, had rented an apartment for them on Euclid Avenue, historian Douglas Brinkley wrote that Rosa, Raymond, and Leona shared a bedroom at Thomas Williamson's house on Fleming Street for the first month they were in Detroit. They then moved to Euclid Avenue, and McCauley and Williamson furnished the apartment for them. Once the family had settled in the apartment, the most important thing for Rosa Parks to do was find a job. But even though Detroit had been good to her brother Sylvester, he called it "Dynamite Detroit,"[3] Rosa Parks had trouble finding a job, and she was not alone. The number of African Americans in Detroit had been increasing since World War I, leading to intense competition for jobs.

During World War I, the *Chicago Defender* had waged an aggressive movement to convince southern blacks to migrate to northern cities. Robert Abbott, the owner and editor of the *Defender*, ran stories portraying the hazards of remaining in the segregated South while pointing out the positive aspects of life in the North. The *Defender* printed job listings and train schedules; it also used editorials, cartoons, and articles with exciting headlines to attract southern blacks. Abbott even went so far as to declare May 15, 1917, the date of the Great Northern Drive. This "Great Migration" resulted in over 1.5 million southern blacks relocating to the North between 1915 and 1925.[4] The sharply increasing black population put pressure on available resources in northern cities, and inevitably clashes between whites and blacks broke out nationwide. These tensions did not abate as time passed. More southern blacks migrated North during World War II, resulting in race riots in

New York, Detroit, and other major cities. Another wave of migration in the postwar period stretched resources even further, and unemployment rose as whites fled the inner cities for the suburbs, taking crucial tax dollars and employment opportunities with them. The black ghetto became a permanent fixture in northern cities, segregated schools became the norm, and residential covenants restricting residential occupancy in certain areas of the city became common. Housing became one battleground. Carl Rowan reported that in Detroit in the 1950s,

> This separate little Negro world also is the area of blight and slums, the remains of a city threatening to decay from the inside while those who might do something about it are fleeing to the suburbs. Inside this horseshoe boulevard are ugly, drab schools that are by any measurement the worst in the city. Here you find junkyards splattered in the midst of residential areas occupied by Negroes who have neither the know-how nor the political pull to secure enforcement of the zoning ordinances. Inside the patches of ugly shacks, most of them studded with "for-rent" signs, you see kerosene burners tucked into the corners of dark, dismal rooms.[5]

While builders constructed about 40,000 dwellings annually in Detroit, because of restrictive covenants, African Americans had access to only about 400 of the units. "Between 1950 and 1956, about 178,000 new homes were constructed in Detroit suburbs. Negroes were permitted to purchase about 730, most of these in a Negro community." In February 1957, violence reigned supreme in an entire Detroit neighborhood as angry whites tried to drive out Mrs. Ethel Watkins "from a house she had purchased about five blocks outside the limits of the so-called Negro neighborhood." Mobs of protestors threw rocks at the house, broke windows, and shouted insults and threats at the white woman who sold the house to Mrs. Watkins. Eventually national news coverage forced Detroit police to quell the riots and protests and Mrs. Watkins moved into the house, but the Cherrylawn incident, as it was known at the time, revealed the depth racial antagonism in the city.[6]

The employment prospects were bleak as well. While in the 1940s black men in the inner city could find good jobs in manufacturing, the decentralization of industry led to a declining number of well-paying,

entry-level manufacturing jobs. Even Michigan's 1956 Fair Employment
Practices law and the efforts of the National Urban League (NUL) and
NAACP had little effect. Industrial suburbanization, technological ad-
vancements, and automation had a chilling effect on black male workers. For example, while black workers made up about 29 percent of the
workers in General Motors Detroit plant in 1960, only 12.5 percent of
the workers in its Livonia plant, a western suburb of Detroit, were African American. Companies preferred to hire workers from the communities living near the factory, which largely excluded inner-city blacks.[7]
Black women found their employment circumscribed as well. Between
1940 and 1960, four-fifths of black women worked in service occupa-
tions, with only slight gains in factory employment during World War II.
In the 1950s and 1960s, the number of black women employed in semi-
skilled factory jobs actually fell.[8] Rosa Parks arrived in Detroit in the
midst of this economic environment.

While she looked for work, Parks also remained active in civil rights,
traveling and speaking to a variety of groups on behalf of the NAACP.
In 1957, she met Alonzo G. Moron, president of the Hampton Institute in Virginia. This was the school that Booker T. Washington
had attended as a young man. At Hampton, Washington studied under
Samuel Chapman Armstrong, a strong proponent of industrial education for blacks. After graduating from Hampton, Washington went on
to found the Tuskegee Institute in 1881, which he modeled on the
Hampton curriculum of industrial education. Moron offered Parks a
job as hostess at the Holly Tree Inn and Dining Hall, a residence and
guesthouse located on the Hampton campus. He wrote:

> I would like very much to have you come to work for us at Hamp-
> ton as hostess at the Holly Tree Inn.... The job is not physically
> taxing, but it does call for someone with sufficient tact, good
> sense, and courtesy to represent the College to the wide variety of
> guests who visit the campus.

As hostess,

Parks was responsible for the operation and supervision of staff
at the Holly Tree Inn and Dining Hall and two other building

occupied by single members of the faculty. She met guests who visited the campus needing accommodations at the Inn and looked after them throughout their stay.

Parks recalled that she had expected that some provision would be made for her husband and mother, but nothing materialized; therefore they stayed in Detroit.[9]

Parks seemed to enjoy her time at Hampton. The Holly Tree Inn offered a particularly pleasant working environment. Housed in a historic American colonial home, the inn provided an office for Parks as well as two small living rooms, a kitchen, and a dining room for faculty and guests. The grounds were scenic and the students Parks met were smart and well mannered. Although her exact salary is unknown, historian Douglas Brinkley wrote that Parks was able to send money to Raymond and her mother in Detroit each month. While Parks worked at Hampton, Raymond attended school to obtain a barber's license in Michigan. He also registered to vote for the first time. After completing his courses, Raymond received his barber's license and took a job as a combination instructor and maintenance man at the barber college in Detroit.[10]

While Parks worked at Hampton, Martin Luther King, Jr., was busy organizing the Southern Christian Leadership Conference (SCLC) and capitalizing on his national recognition by writing *Stride Toward Freedom: The Montgomery Story*, describing how maids, washerwomen, laborers, cooks, and other African Americans in Montgomery stayed off the buses until the U.S. Supreme Court ruled in their favor. The book detailed Rosa Parks's arrest and E. D. Nixon's role in the protest, and it praised Parks for her role in the boycott. Harper and Brothers scheduled publication for the end of September 1958. The publicity campaign began by bringing King to Harlem to appear on *The Today Show* on September 17 and to sign the books for eager readers at Blumstein's Department Store on September 20. As about 50 people waited in line, a well-dressed black woman in sequined glasses asked the man at the desk if he was Martin Luther King. After learning that he was indeed King, 42-year-old Izola Ware Curry walked up to him and said, "Luther King, I've been after you for five years." She then took out a razor-sharp Japanese letter opener and stabbed King in the left side of his chest. Shocked, King remained seated in the chair with the letter opener lodged in his chest until the ambulance arrived. During a four-hour surgery at Harlem Hospital, Dr. Aubré Menard removed the letter opener, which had lodged between King's lung and heart, dangerously close to his aorta.[11]

By the time his surgery was over, the news of the stabbing flashed across both radio and television broadcasts. Parks was reading her personally autographed copy of *Stride Toward Freedom*, which she had just received, when she heard the news. Parks wrote that King's stabbing profoundly shocked her. She had, she noted, become hysterical on hearing about it, and she was greatly relieved on learning that he had survived the surgery and would recover.[12]

The faculty and staff at Hampton were pleased that Rosa Parks was a member of their family. In May 1958, they awarded Parks "The Women's Senate of Hampton Institutes Certificate of Merit" in honor of her work in civil rights. Nevertheless, in December, Parks returned to Detroit for the Christmas holidays and decided not to return to the Holly Tree Inn. She loved her job, but Moron had promised her housing for her family, and the promise went unfulfilled. Parks made efforts to find housing for all three of them, and she attempted to get Raymond a job at a nearby barbershop for blacks, but she did not succeed. An apartment at the Holly Tree Inn Annex that she inquired about was never made available. Raymond and Leona did not do well in Rosa's absence, and Rosa was not well either. Eventually the strains of separation proved to be too much for her. While she was in Detroit that December, she saw a doctor, had minor surgery, and determined that she would have to stay in Detroit. Parks nevertheless recalled that she experienced some regret at having to leave a job she enjoyed and the pleasant atmosphere at Hampton, and that her employers there were reluctant to lose her.[13]

After Parks returned to Detroit, she worked as a seamstress in Leonard and May Stockton's small downtown clothing factory. From 1959 through 1964, Parks sewed cotton aprons and skirts, often for 10 hours a day at the Stockton Sewing Company. Her earnings were based on "piecework"; that is, she was paid for each piece completed, a common system used by clothing factories to pay female workers during the 1950s and 1960s. Parks's 75-cent rate gave her a steady income and enabled her to support her husband and mother. According to historian Douglas Brinkley, in 1961, Parks met Elaine Eason Steele at the Stockton Sewing Company. Born in Tuskegee, Elaine moved to Detroit when she was six years old. Her father, Frank C. Eason, who had been a Tuskegee Airman, owned a collision business, and her mother, Bertha Wallace Eason, taught school before moving to Detroit. While a student at Cass Technical High School, Steele worked after school at the Stockton Sewing Company. Brinkley writes that Steele was astounded to discover that Rosa Parks, the civil rights heroine she was learning about in her history class, was her co-worker. According to Brinkley, Steele recalled that Parks was "so sweet and nice and showed me how to use the power-industrial Singer machine—how to place the garment under the needle just right."[14] Steele worked at the company for only five days before Leonard Stockton fired her for low output. Nevertheless, after she graduated from Cass, Steele stayed in touch with Parks, who, according to Brinkley, treated Steele as the daughter she never had.[15] In addition to her paid work, Parks spent time at family reunions with her brother, Sylvester, his wife, Daisy, and babysitting her 13 nieces and nephews. The family was very proud of Parks; the children often boasting of their aunt and telling their friends they were a "civil rights family."[16]

Parks continued her civil rights activism as well. She joined the local NAACP chapter—she was a lifetime member of the NAACP—and spoke at many chapter meetings nationwide, including a 1957 meeting at the 8th Street Baptist Church in Kansas City, Kansas. She returned to the Highlander Folk School to participate on a panel entitled "The South Thinking Ahead" for the United Packing House Workers. Parks was active in local civic groups as well, including the 32–3300 Virginia Park Block Club, which addressed neighborhood conditions, and the Q Street Block Club. The main goals of these neighborhood groups were to maintain the physical appearance of neighborhoods and welcome new neighbors, but the members also worked to encourage voter registration, help parents to keep children in school, make neighborhood residents aware of current problems, and promote active leadership. Parks was an avid reader, keeping up with current events, and not simply through mainstream newspapers. She received newsletters from the American Friends Service Committee and kept back issues of the *Quaker Service Bulletin*.[17]

In 1957, the *Chicago Defender* honored Parks by placing her name on its 1956 Honor Roll of Democracy, and she was an honorary member of SCLC as well. Parks attended the SCLC's annual conventions and retreats whenever possible. Since the Montgomery boycott, King became widely regarded as black America's preeminent spokesman, and the SCLC had become the principal civil rights organization in the South. The Montgomery Bus Boycott brought attention to King and increased his resolve to use nonviolent direct action as the only practical approach for attaining equality. In fact, the SCLC leadership considered the training of new political activists in nonviolent tactics a priority. Although a number of civil rights activists, including Rosa Parks and E. D. Nixon, were not fully committed to nonviolence, King insisted on maintaining this strategy. SCLC actions aimed at desegregation included such tactics as class-action lawsuits, boycotts against merchants who would not desegregate their stores, sit-ins, rallies and marches, and voter registration drives. By 1962, the SCLC had initiated Operation Breadbasket and the Citizenship Education Program, an expansion of Septima Clark's Highlander-inspired Citizenship Schools. The SCLC sponsored these programs to improve African Americans' economic status, increase literacy, educate new voters, and encourage community organizing programs.[18]

While the SCLC was organizing, the civil rights movement took on a life of its own. On February 1, 1960, Ezell Blair, Jr., Franklin Eugene McCain, Joseph Alfred McNeil, and David Leinail Richmond, students at North Carolina Agricultural and Technical College (A&T) decided to test the segregation laws in Greensboro, North Carolina. They entered the Elm Street Woolworth's at 4 P.M. to purchase school supplies and other items. After paying for their purchases, they went to the lunch counter and ordered coffee. Refused service, the four remained in their seats until closing at 5 P.M. This first Greensboro sit-in was not spontaneous; the students had thoroughly planned and executed the protest; they had gained the support of white allies and made sure the media would cover the sit-in. The next day, 29 students continued the sit-in; then there were 63, then 300—and white students from surrounding colleges joined the black students. By the third week in February, the sit-ins had spread, and within a few months, the students had succeeded in desegregating lunch counters across the South.[19] After the student protests began, Ella Baker arranged an organizing meeting at Shaw University for the protesters in order to help them keep their forward momentum. Over 200 students attended the meeting, and after a series of contentious discussions, the student demonstrators formed the Student Non-Violent Coordinating Committee (SNCC).[20] In the following years, SNCC would go on to hold a series of controversial voter registration drives and protests against segregation throughout the South.

Meanwhile, in the fall of 1962, Rosa Parks traveled to Birmingham, Alabama, to attend the SCLC's annual convention. Parks described what happened: King was making his closing remarks when a white man in the audience jumped up and rushed the stage. The man punched King in the face so hard it spun him backward. Before anyone could react, the man hit King a second time. At first King tried to shield himself, but he then dropped his hands and looked directly at his assailant, putting him off balance long enough for others to get between them. King insisted that no one touch his attacker and began speaking softly to him as he and several others led the man off the stage. After the attack, Parks recalled going backstage to offer King her remedy for a headache—two aspirins and a Coca-Cola. King later told the audience that the man told him he was a member of the American Nazi Party and was angry because black entertainer Sammy Davis, Jr., had recently married a white woman. In her autobiography, Parks noted that King declined to press charges against his assailant, concluding that King's conduct proved that his commitment to nonviolence surpassed even his natural instinct to ward off a physical attack.[21] In the spring of 1963, Birmingham would test King's commitment to nonviolence on a much larger scale.

On April 3, 1963, the SCLC began Project C—the Birmingham desegregation campaign. Protestors filled the downtown area, marched, and held sit-ins at department stores and restaurants. On Good Friday, police arrested Martin Luther King, Jr., and on Easter Sunday, police brutally beat protestors and then took them into custody. On May 2, more than a thousand African American children entered the protest. They began their march from the Sixth Street Baptist Church, and as they approached downtown, police arrested hundreds and took them to jail. Police commissioner Eugene "Bull" Connor then told the local police and fire department to use high-pressure fire hoses, police dogs, and their nightsticks to end the protest. Reporters and photographers filled the newspapers with images of the attack on the protestors. Television reporters and cameramen televised the images, triggering worldwide outrage. White ministers criticized King for his use of civil disobedience, calling it "unwise and untimely." They then appealed "to both our white and Negro citizenry to observe the principles of law and order and common sense." King responded from his cell, in his now famous "Letter from Birmingham Jail." King called into question the clergy's charge of impatience and of the "extreme" level of the campaign's actions. "For years now, I have heard the word 'Wait!'" King wrote. "This 'Wait' has almost always meant 'Never.'" King justified the tactic of civil disobedience by stating that "just as the Bible's Shadrach, Meshach, and Abednego refused to obey Nebuchadnezzar's unjust laws," he refused to submit to laws and injunctions that were "used to maintain segregation and to deny citizens the First-Amendment privilege of peaceful assembly and protest." King insisted,

> I submit that an individual who breaks a law that conscience tells him is unjust, and who willingly accepts the penalty of imprisonment in order to arouse the conscience of the community over its injustice, is in reality expressing the highest respect for law.[22]

Rosa Parks was not in Birmingham to take part in the protests, but she did work with King again. In June 1963, King came to Detroit to hold his Great March to Freedom, in reality a rehearsal for the March on Washington to be held that August. According to historian Douglas Brinkley, Rosa Parks was at King's side during the march down Woodward Avenue to Cobo Hall for most of the afternoon. It was during this demonstration that King first invoked his now famous "I Have a Dream" refrain. King spoke of the effectiveness of nonviolence as a tactic to achieve equality, the rampant segregation endured by blacks in the North, and the shortcomings of black separatism. He then told the audience "we ought to march to Washington more than 100,000 in order to say ... that we are determined, and in order to engage in a nonviolent protest to keep this issue before the conscience of the nation." At the march King elaborated his dream for America, "I have a dream. It is a dream deeply rooted in the American dream."

I have a dream that one day, right down in Georgia and Mississippi and Alabama, the sons of former slaves and the sons of former slave owners will be able to live together as brothers.

I have a dream this afternoon that one day, one day little white children and little Negro children will be able to join hands as brothers and sisters...

I have a dream this afternoon that there will be a day that we will no longer face the atrocities that Emmett Till had to face or Medgar Evers had to face, that all men can live with dignity.

I have a dream this afternoon that my four little children, that my four little children will not come up in the same young days that I came up within, but they will be judged on the basis of the content of their character, not the color of their skin.[23]

For Parks, the most inspiring moment came when King, speaking in Detroit in June 1963, said, "I have a dream this afternoon that one day right here in Detroit, Negroes will be able to buy a house or rent a house anywhere that their money will carry them and they will be able to get a job."[24] African Americans in Detroit could identify with this line because it addressed the issues they faced daily in the urban North.

The next time Rosa Parks would see King would be on August 28, 1963, at the March on Washington for Jobs and Freedom. The idea for a March on Washington originated in 1941, when A. Philip Randolph, president of the Brotherhood of Sleeping Car Porters, called for a march on meant to pressure President Roosevelt to guarantee jobs for black men and women in wartime industries. When Roosevelt signed Executive Order 8802, creating the Fair Employment Practices Commission (FEPC) and increasing African Americans' access to wartime jobs, Randolph called off the march. King resurrected the idea in June 1963, after President Kennedy made a historic civil rights speech asking for a new civil rights bill, and after white supremacists had assassinated Mississippi NAACP leader Medgar Evers outside his home. The 1963 demonstration, organized by A. Philip Randolph and Bayard Rustin, attracted more than 250,000 people. It was undeniably the largest civil rights demonstration in the United States up to that time, designed as a peaceful protest to promote civil rights and economic equality.

Marchers walked down Constitution and Independence Avenues and gathered around the reflecting pool before the Lincoln Monument for speeches, songs, and prayers. SCLC invited Rosa Parks, Septima Clark, Ella Baker, and several other prominent women to take part in the events. Parks was soon disappointed, however, by how the men were discriminating against the women. The men relegated the wives of male leaders—including Coretta Scott King and female activists such as Parks, Clark, and Baker—to a separate procession and did not invite the women to speak in the program.[25] A. Philip Randolph, perhaps because he sensed that the women were disgruntled because of the slight or perhaps because he knew that the women were largely responsible for initiating the movement, arranged a Tribute to Women at the last moment. During the tribute, as Randolph called their names, Parks and the other prominent women activists stood to be recognized, but only the voices of singers Marian Anderson and Mahalia Jackson were heard as they sang to the crowd. Parks later noted in her autobiography that the other women present were not given a public voice at the march, commenting that although women would no longer be content with such a minor role, at that time women's rights had not yet emerged as a popular movement.[26]

Parks was only partially correct. Although the idea of women's rights was not then widely accepted, that had not stopped women such as Sojourner Truth, Elizabeth Cady Stanton, Susan B. Anthony, Anna Julia Cooper, and Ida B. Wells from fighting for women's rights in the 19th century. In the 20th century, women such as Mary Church Terrell, Lucy Laney, Carrie Chapman Catt, Alice Paul, Charlotte Hawkins Brown, and Mary McLeod Bethune kept the struggle alive. In fact, Parks was among those fighting for women's rights as well. Since 1954, Parks had maintained a membership in the National Association of Colored Women (NACW), founded by Mary Church Terrell. The NACW worked to improve the lives of disadvantaged African Americans, with many of it programs focusing on job training, equal wages, and child care. However, the NACW had a larger political agenda as well, which called public attention to issues such as lynching, prison conditions, and segregated transportation. In addition, local chapters helped to organize voter registration drives and promote the education of women and young people through local, state, and regional workshops, seminars, and scholarships. As a member of this group, Parks had to have been aware that the NACW endeavored to "obtain for African American women the opportunity of reaching the highest levels in all fields of human endeavor."[27] In other words, it sought not only women's rights but also women's equality.

In 1955, Parks joined another women's group—the National Council of Negro Women (NCNW). In 1935, Mary McLeod Bethune called together leaders of black women's organizations to create an umbrella organization that would coordinate black women's efforts for racial justice and equality. Bethune envisioned NCNW as a clearinghouse, assisting in networking and coalition building while also creating political strength and solidarity and preparing black women to take public office. The NCNW encouraged and supported women's independent political action.[28] Parks's membership would certainly have exposed her to other women who would serve as a support system for her political activism.

Her experience with gender discrimination at the March on Washington may have spurred her interest in joining additional groups promoting women's equality as well. In 1963, Parks became a founding member of the United Sisterhood of Michigan. This interracial, inter-religious women's group was dedicated to "promoting love, fellowship and better human relations." Its motto spoke to the founding members desire for authentic gender equality—"Brotherhood and Sisterhood a Reality 365 Days."[29] Parks joined other women's groups as well. By August 1964, she was working with Women United for Freedom and Justice and was active with the 13th District Democratic Women, a group dedicated to electing more women in all of Detroit's political districts. Parks joined station WXYZ Women's Advisory Committee, a group formed to address women's concerns within the media, including the addition of more women's news features, countering sexist ideas presented in the media, and hiring more women in the media.[30] In 1964, Parks became a member of the Women's Public Affairs Committee of 1000. According to the literature for the committee, it was a nonpartisan and nonsectarian group. The main focus of the committee was to "work for love, harmony and understanding; promote goodwill among women of all racial, religious and ethnic backgrounds; seek equality for all and a better understanding of American history, laws and ideals in order to achieve it." Jeanetta Welch Brown, a prominent black activist in Detroit and president of the local NCNW chapter, led the committee. In April 1965, the committee paid tribute to Parks with a testimonial dinner honoring her work in civil rights. By 1968, Parks had expanded her activism on behalf of women's equality. She joined the Detroit branch of the Women's International League for Peace and Freedom, which focused on issues such as equal education, teachers' pensions, public library legislation, tax reform, disarmament, nonviolence, child care, campaign reform, economic development, and human rights. By 1971, Parks was service as one of six vice-presidents of the group. And in 1974, she became one of four honorary chairwomen of the Women's Conference of Concerns, an umbrella organization organized by Detroit Councilwoman Erma Henderson. According to the literature, the group's individual and organizational members were

dedicated to finding new and better responses to all aspects of our society be it education, social services, civil rights and liberties, land use, communications, health, criminal justice, youth, political awareness, and above all, in creative awareness of ourselves as women and in our relationship to each other and to the total community.[31]

After August 1963, in other words, Rosa Parks became more active in women's groups and as a public and vocal supporter of women's equality.

Parks did not abandon her civil rights work, however. She believed it was important that all citizens understand their government and their rights under the Constitution. She spoke at the seventh annual SCLC conference in Richmond, Virginia, and was excited to learn about the different ways in which African Americans were organizing and demonstrating across the South. Finally, change was coming. Parks knew that the demonstrations, marches, sit-ins, and other protests would not automatically change the racial attitudes of many white southerners, but she did know that these events were affecting the politicians in Washington. After President Kennedy's assassination on November 22, 1963, Vice President Lyndon B. Johnson became the 36th president of the United States. Although a southerner by birth, Johnson pushed Kennedy's proposed civil rights act through Congress. He had been spurred on by the March on Washington and by the September 15, 1963, bombing at Birmingham's Sixteenth Street Baptist Church, which killed four young girls—Cynthia Wesler, Carole Robertson, and Addie Mae Collins, all aged 14, and 11-year-old Denise McNair.[32] The Civil Rights Act of 1964—Public Law 82–352 (78 Stat. 241)—was the most far-reaching piece of legislation in relationship to black equality since Reconstruction.

Legislators specifically designed the Civil Rights Act of 1964 to address several issues. First, it enforced the constitutional right to vote. Second, it gave district courts the power to issue injunctions to end discrimination in public places. Further, it permitted the attorney general to initiate lawsuits to protect all citizens' constitutional rights in public facilities and public education, and it extended the Commission on Civil Rights. Finally, it took measures to prevent discrimination in programs receiving government funds and established a Commission on Equal Employment Opportunity. Section 703 (a) made it illegal for an employer to "fail or refuse to hire or to discharge any individual, or otherwise to discriminate against any individual with respect to his compensation, terms, conditions or privileges or employment, because of such individual's race, color, religion, sex, or national origin."[33] Although the act could not change a person's attitudes, it did regulate behavior and clearly spelled out the consequences of ignoring it.

In 1964, Rosa Parks met John Conyers, an African American attorney born and raised in Detroit. From 1958 to 1961, he worked as a legislative assistant for Congressman John Dingle and then served as a referee in the Michigan Workmen's Compensation Department. Conyers was active in the civil rights movement as one of the founders of the National Lawyers Committee for Civil Rights Under Law; he traveled to the south as well to work with the SCLC. He opposed the Vietnam War, fought for the right of the residents of Washington, D.C., to gain congressional representation, and supported the effort to lower the voting age to 18. In 1964, Conyers ran for Congress as the representative for Michigan's First Congressional District and won. Rosa Parks recalled that Conyers had requested her endorsement and that she had given it, since she approved of his positions and his legislative plans.[34] Parks regarded Conyers as an important political leader because he not only fought for civil rights, peace, and economic justice but also supported bringing an end to the death penalty, all causes that she supported.

In an interview, Conyers remembered that he had met Parks through the SCLC before she came to Detroit. When he decided to run for Congress, Conyers recalled,

> it so happened that she was also coming to my campaign meetings.... And to our great delight, she was very quiet, but she would come and she would help us.... I said that when I won this seat, the first thing I would do is offer her a position on my staff, if she would accept.... to my honor and delight, she did accept. And we were happy to have her in my original staff.[35]

Conyers was as good as his word. After his election, he offered Parks a job in his Detroit office as a receptionist and office assistant. She accepted the offer, left her job at the Stockton Sewing Company, and on March 1, 1965, began working as a member of Representative Conyers's

Parks worked in Congressman Conyers's Detroit office from March 1965 until her retirement in 1988. She was photographed at work on May 28, 1971. (AP Photo/Jim McKnight)

staff. She remained a part of that staff until her retirement in 1988.[36] According to historian Douglas Brinkley, Parks was not only a diligent and efficient employee but also a political asset. Conyers recalled, "Rosa Parks was so famous that people would come by my office to meet her, not me."[37]

Even though Parks now had a full-time job as a staffer in Conyers's office, she did not disregard the growing civil rights movement, and Conyers encouraged her ongoing participation. In March 1965, civil rights leaders called for a march from Selma to Montgomery, Alabama, to demonstrate the need for a national voting rights bill. In many southern states, registrars still denied African Americans the right to vote. This was most prevalent in states with large black populations—such as Mississippi, Alabama, and Georgia—although these were not the only states to disenfranchise blacks. In the summer of 1964, the SNCC launched a voter registration drive in Mississippi, which they called Freedom Summer. Young activists such as James Farmer traveled to northern college campuses to recruit and train white students in nonviolent direct-action tactics; these students would then come to Mississippi and help blacks to register. Thousands of young, idealistic northern students volunteered and trained for the program, while white supremacist groups in the South geared up to stop them. Violence was inevitable, and it came swiftly. White supremacist groups firebombed or burned 37 black churches and 30 black homes and businesses during that summer. Police arrested more than a thousand black and white volunteers, and the police or white mobs severely beat at least eighty activists. On June 21, 1964, three civil rights activists—James Chaney, a veteran African American activist; Michael Schwerner, a white veteran activist; and Andrew Goodman, a northern white college student—left SNCC headquarters in Neshoba County to investigate a church bombing in Philadelphia, Mississippi. It was the last time anyone saw them alive. The next day their burned-out station wagon was found in Bogue Chitto Swamp, but it took until August to find their bodies, which were buried in an earthen dam near Philadelphia, Mississippi. Chaney had been savagely beaten, while Schwerner and Goodman had each been shot once in the chest. Since two of the murdered men were white, these murders attracted much more attention than previous attacks, in which the victims had been all black. Mississippi authorities never arrested anyone in the case, but the federal government did prosecute seven men on federal conspiracy charges; the jury acquitted seven others and three had mistrials. The longest sentence imposed was six years.[38]

Several civil rights leaders called for a 54-mile march from Selma to Montgomery to dramatize the inequality in voter registration. Governor George Wallace warned the demonstrators that he would stop the march, but Wallace's threats did not stop it. On Sunday, March 7, the protesters wound their way through the streets of Selma and moved across the Edmund Pettus Bridge, where Alabama state troopers waited. The marchers refused to disband, and the troopers advanced, beating the marchers with their nightsticks, blinding them with tear gas, and trampling the fallen protesters with their horses. The marchers tried to flee across the bridge, but the troopers pursued them, beating and trampling them. Television coverage of "Bloody Sunday" drew national outrage. On March 15, in a televised address, President Johnson introduced his Voting Rights Act and vowed that it would become law. African American activists had won part of the battle—voting rights legislation would go to Congress, but there was no guarantee that it would pass. So the demonstrators pressed on; they were not going to let the violence deter them. Additional demonstrators joined the march, and on March 21, the protest resumed. But this time President Johnson ordered 1,800 Alabama national guardsmen to protect the demonstrators.[39]

In Detroit, Rosa Parks marched down Woodward Avenue with hundreds of others in sympathy for the Selma protestors, and when King called her and asked if she would come to Alabama to join the demonstrators, she quickly agreed. Parks did not have the money to get to Alabama, so she asked a friend's husband if he would approach the United Auto Workers (UAW) union for the money. The UAW agreed and two union officials accompanied her throughout the trip.[40] According to historian Taylor Branch, by the time the demonstrators were just outside of Montgomery, the marchers were on edge. Demonstrators fought among themselves about who would lead the line into Montgomery. Marshals distributed orange vests to the 300 people, mainly Selma High School students, who had marched the entire 50 miles. This group was to lead the nearly 12,000 demonstrators into Montgomery. Some of the newcomers demanded vests as well claiming that their sponsors told them "Dr. King wanted us to march with him." The young people asserted themselves. One 17-year-old said, "I didn't see any of you fellows in Selma, and I didn't see you on the way to Montgomery. Ain't nobody going to get in front of me but Dr. King." Marshals placed the students wearing the orange vests at the head of the line as an honor vanguard, next in line were the photographers, and then King and the other leaders. Rosa Parks joined the march on March 25, outside of Montgomery and "found herself shoved several times to the sidewalk, where she stood until a marshal who knew her came along to make a fuss about getting her in the march." After Parks's more than 8 years in Detroit, many of the younger marchers had never heard of her and simply did not recognize her. "It seemed like such a short time that I had been out of Alabama, but so many young people had grown up in that time. They didn't know who I was and couldn't care less about me because they didn't know me,"[41] she later remarked. Parks recalled, "I *was* in it, but they put me out." She dropped back in the crowd, but when some of the older activists saw her, they asked her to walk with them. Still, over the course of the day, she was sent back four or five times. When the demonstrators finally neared the capitol building, an SCLC veteran took her arm and pulled her to the front of the line. As the line of protestors moved forward, some whites who were harassing the demonstrators recognized Parks jeered at her. When the line of marchers finally reached the capitol building, the leaders asked Parks to speak.[42] There was deafening applause. Parks told historian Douglas Brinkley that she told the crowd about Highlander Folk School, what she learned there, and to disregard the propaganda about the Communist support of the school. Taylor Branch wrote that Parks spoke about hiding from the Klan as a small child. Then she softly said, "My family was deprived of the land that they owned. I am handicapped in every way." Her voice faltered, and she stepped away from the microphones.[43]

The Selma-to-Montgomery March achieved its goal. On August 3, 1965, the House of Representatives passed the Voting Rights Bill; the next day the Senate passed the identical bill. On August 6, President Johnson, his cabinet, and invited guests crowded into the President's Room in the Senate building to witness Johnson's signing of the Voting Rights Act of 1965. Johnson called the day "a triumph for freedom," recalled the "outrage of Selma" on the Edmund Pettus Bridge, and praised the vote as "the most powerful instrument ever devised by man for breaking down injustice."[44] The act prohibited any state from denying or circumscribing the right to vote based on literacy tests. In addition, the act prohibited any state from implementing changes in their voting laws until the U.S. Attorney General or the U.S. District Court for the District of Columbia could determine if the changes would discriminate against any group of voters. The U.S. Attorney General could also appoint a federal examiner in any county to review the qualifications set for voting, and federal observers could be sent to those counties to oversee the voting process.[45] After he signed the bill, Johnson handed out signing pens to legislators, civil rights leaders, and invited guests, including Rosa Parks.[46] Soon after Johnson signed the Voting Rights Act, federal examiners began conducting voter registration. By the end of 1965, almost 250,000 new black voters had registered, and African Americans had won seats in the Georgia legislature and in city councils of several southern states.[47]

African American activists had worked to institute change in America through sit-ins, marches, boycotts, and demonstrations. They had succeeded in making legal changes with the passage of the Civil Rights Act of 1964 and the Voting Rights Act of 1965. Nevertheless, as President Dwight D. Eisenhower said, integration required a change in people's hearts and minds, a process that could take generations. By 1966, the leadership in the civil rights movement was changing. Younger, more militant activists were taking charge and they were unwilling to wait for whites to changes their hearts and minds. After 1967, the movement began to splinter. King's followers believed in integration and dismissed the use of violence as both impractical and immoral. Younger activists followed a different path—one based on revolution and "black power."

NOTES

1. Rosa Parks with Jim Haskins, *My Story* (New York: Penguin Books, 1992), 161; Douglas Brinkley, *Rosa Parks; A Life* (New York: Penguin Books, 2000), 174; Rosa L. Parks Papers, Walter Reuther Archives of Labor and Urban Affairs, Wayne State University, box 1.

2. Patricia Sullivan, ed., *Freedom Writer: Virginia Foster Durr, Letters from the Civil Rights Years* (New York: Routledge, 2003), 152.

3. Brinkley, *Rosa Parks*, 177; Parks, *My Story*, 161.

4. "The Chicago Defender," http://www.pbs.org/blackpress/news_bios/defender.html (accessed August 20, 2009).

5. Carl T. Rowan, "The Negro in the North," *Saturday Evening Post* 230, no. 16 (October 19, 1957): 86.

6. Ibid., 86–88.

7. Michael B. Katz, *"The Underclass Debate": Views from History* (Princeton: NJ: Princeton University Press, 1992), 109.

8. Thomas J. Sugrue, *The Origins of the Urban Crisis: Race and Inequality in Postwar Detroit* (Princeton, NJ: Princeton University Press, 2005), 275–76.

9. "HU Mourns the Loss of Rosa Parks," http://www.hamptonu.edu/news/102605_27_rosa_parks.htm (accessed August 21, 2009); Parks, *My Story*, 162; Brinkley, *Rosa Parks*, 178.

10. Marcia M. Greenlee, "Interview with Rosa McCauley Parks" on August 22 and 23, 1978, in *The Black Woman Oral History Project*, vol. 8, ed. Ruth Edmonds Hill (Westport, CT: Meckler, 1991), 256; Parks, *My Story*, 162–63; Brinkley, *Rosa Parks*, 179–80.

11. Stephen B. Oates, *Let the Trumpet Sound: A Life of Martin Luther King, Jr.* (New York: Harper Perennial, 1994), 138; Hugh Pearson, *When Harlem Nearly Killed King: The 1958 Stabbing of Dr. Martin Luther King, Jr.* (New York: Seven Stories Press, 2004), 9, 23.

12. Parks, *My Story*, 163.

13. Rosa L. Parks Papers, Walter Reuther Archives of Labor and Urban Affairs, Wayne State University, box 1, folder 3; Parks, *My Story*, 163–64.

14. Elaine Eason Steele Biography, http://www.rosaparks.org/index.php?option=com_content&view=article&id=24&Itemid=34 (accessed August 21, 2009); Parks, *My Story*, 164; Brinkley, *Rosa Parks*, 181–82.

15. Brinkley, *Rosa Parks*, 182.

16. Helen O'Neill, "Activist's Family Ponders Her Legacy," *Los Angeles Times*, (December 12, 2004), A1.

17. Rosa L. Parks Papers, Walter Reuther Archives of Labor and Urban Affairs, Wayne State University, box 1, folders 1, 3, 4, and 5.

18. "Southern Christian Leadership Conference," *The New Georgia Encyclopedia*, http://www.georgiaencyclopedia.org/nge/Article.jsp?id=h-2743 (accessed August 23, 2009).

19. William Henry Chafe, *Civilities and Civil Rights: Greensboro, North Carolina, and the Black Struggle for Freedom* (New York: Oxford University Press, 1981); North Carolina History Project, "Greensboro Sit-In," http://www.northcarolinahistory.org/encyclopedia/299/entry (accessed August 23, 2009).

20. Joann Grant, *Ella Baker: Freedom Bound* (New York: John Wiley & Sons, 1998), 125–31.

21. Parks, *My Story*, 164–65; Brinkley, *Rosa Parks*, 183–84.

22. "White Clergymen Urge Local Negroes to Withdraw from Demonstrations," *Birmingham News* (April 13, 1963); The Birmingham Desegregation Campaign, http://www.amistadresource.org/civil_rights_era/birmingham_desegregation_campaign.html (accessed August 23, 2009); Children's Crusade, http://mlk-kpp01.stanford.edu/index.php/encyclopedia/encyclopedia/enc_childrens_crusade/ (accessed August 23, 2009); Martin Luther King, Jr., *Why We Can't Wait* (New York: Mentor, 1964); David Garrow, *Bearing the Cross* (New York: Harper Perennial Modern Classics, 2004); Taylor Branch, *Parting the Waters: America in the King Years 1954–63* (New York: Simon & Schuster, 1989).

23. "Speech at the Great March on Detroit," http://mlk-kpp01.stanford.edu/index.php/kingpapers/article/speech_at_the_great_march_on_detroit/ (accessed August 24, 2009).

24. Brinkley, *Rosa Parks*, 184.

25. Parks, *My Story*, 165; Brinkley, *Rosa Parks*, 185; "The March on Washington," http://www.core-online.org/History/washington_march.htm (accessed August 24, 2009); "1963 March on Washington: 'Freedom' The Demands, The Pledge, The Prayer," http://forum-network.org/node/1267 (accessed August 24, 2009).

26. Parks, *My Story*, 166.

27. National Association of Colored Women, http://www.nacwc.org/about/objectives.php (accessed August 24, 2009); The Rise and Fall of Jim Crow, http://www.pbs.org/wnet/jimcrow/stories_org_nacw.html (accessed August 24, 2009).

28. Joyce A. Hanson, *Mary McLeod Bethune and Black Women's Political Activism* (Columbia, MO: University of Missouri Press, 2003); National Council of Negro Women, http://www.ncnw.org/index.htm (accessed August 24, 2009).

29. Rosa L. Parks Papers, box 1, folder 2.

30. Rosa L. Parks Papers, box 4, folder 13.

31. Rosa L. Parks Papers, box 4, folder 13–17.

32. 16th Street Baptist Church Bombing, http://www.npr.org/tem plates/story/story.php?storyId=1431932 (accessed August 25, 2009).

33. Transcript of Civil Rights Act (1964), http://www.ourdocuments. gov/doc.php?doc=97&page=transcript (accessed August 24, 2009); The Civil Rights Act of 1964 and the Equal Employment Opportunity Commission, http://www.archives.gov/education/lessons/civil-rights-act/ (accessed August 24, 2009).

34. Bruce A. Ragsdale and Joel D. Treese, *Black Americans in Congress, 1870–1989* (Washington: Diane Publishing, 2000), 25–26; Parks, *My Story*, 176.

35. Amy Goodman, "John Conyers on Rosa Parks: 'She Earned the Title as Mother of the Civil Rights Movement,'" Democracy Now, http://www.democracynow.org/2005/10/25/john_conyers_on_rosa_parks_she (accessed August 24, 2009.).

36. Parks, *My Story*, 176.

37. Brinkley, *Rosa Parks*, 188.

38. Doug McAdams, *Freedom Summer* (New York: Oxford University Press, 1990), 35–70.

39. Selma to Montgomery March, Martin Luther King Papers, http://mlk-kpp01.stanford.edu/index.php/encyclopedia/encyclopedia/enc_selma_to_montgomery_march/ (accessed August 24, 2009).

40. Brinkley, *Rosa Parks*, 195–96.

41. Ibid., 198.

42. Ibid., 199.

43. Ibid.; Taylor Branch, *At Canaan's Edge* (New York: Simon and Schuster, 2006), 160–64.

44. Branch, *At Canaan's Edge*, 276.

45. The Voting Rights Act of 1965, http://www.usdoj.gov/crt/voting/intro/intro_b.php (accessed August 25, 2009).

46. Branch, *At Canaan's Edge*, 277.

47. John Hope Franklin and Alfred A. Moss, *From Slavery to Freedom*, 8th ed. (New York: McGraw Hill, 2000), 542.

Chapter 8

CONTINUING ACTIVISM

Violence, Martin Luther King, Jr., once said, was "both impractical and immoral." Nonviolent resistance, he believed, was "the only morally and practically sound method open to oppressed people in their struggle for freedom."[1] Not everyone agreed with King. As much as Rosa Parks admired King, she never believed that nonviolence should be the only response to segregation. She recalled that "Dr. King used to say that black people should receive brutality with love, and I believed this was a goal to work for. But I couldn't reach that point in my mind at all."[2] This statement would have shocked anyone who did not know Parks very well, but for those closest to her, it made perfect sense. Her childhood friend Johnnie Mae Carr described Parks as "quiet, but strong-willed, brave without braggadocio, and genuinely kind but nobody's fool."[3] In an interview at the time of Parks's death, Congressman John Conyers said,

> And I can't help but marvel at the fact that Rosa Parks essentially had a saint-like quality. And I use that term advisedly, because she never raised her voice. She was not an emotional person in terms of expressing anger or rage or vindictiveness. But she was resolute.[4]

Conyers told historian Douglas Brinkley that Parks "had a heavy progressive streak about her that was uncharacteristic for a neat, religious, demure, churchgoing lady."[5] Parks summed up her views on nonviolence in her autobiography:

> When I think back to the times of my growing up and the problems we had, I realize we didn't know anything about nonviolence.... We always felt that if you talked violently and said what you would do if they did something to you, that did more good than nonviolence.... I just couldn't accept being pushed even at the cost of my life. I was raised to be proud, and it worked for me to stand up aggressively for myself.... Most of the black people in Montgomery had similar feelings. On an individual level, nonviolence could be mistaken for cowardice.... To this day, I am not an absolute supporter of nonviolence in all situations.[6]

Rosa Parks did indeed have a militant side. In the 1960s, Parks embraced black nationalism and became a great admirer of Malcolm X, although she was not comfortable with his early messages of hatred for whites. Before Malcolm X made a pilgrimage to Mecca, he often spoke about whites as devils or snakes. In 1963, Malcolm spoke to a crowd of four thousand in Chicago, telling them, "The white man is the greatest teacher of hate that ever walked the earth."[7] He then condoned integration, criticizing African Americans who championed integration—calling them Uncle Toms who were willing to accept "a few bones" at the whim of the white man. While Parks could not accept these beliefs, she did see value in the Nation of Islam's condemnation of smoking, drinking, and drug use.[8] Historian Timothy Tyson recalls his first meeting with Rosa Parks:

> I met Rosa Parks at the funeral of Robert F. Williams, who had fought the Ku Klux Klan in North Carolina with a machine gun in the late 1950s and then fled to Cuba, and had been a kind of international revolutionary icon of black power. Ms. Parks delivered the eulogy at his funeral.[9]

Parks was not alone in embracing some facets of black nationalism. In 1963, SNCC chairman Charles McDew invited members of the

Nation of Islam to speak at a SNCC meeting in Albany, Georgia. "Did the people like it? Man, you better believe it," said McDew. According to McDew, by this time some civil rights activists were questioning whether integration should be the goal for the movement—integration meant accepting white society's norms. Many young African Americans now believed that they should be working for *desegregation*, not integration.[10]

By 1964, Malcolm X had split with Elijah Muhammad, head of the Nation of Islam. In letters sent to civil rights leaders Bayard Rustin and Reverend Milton A. Galimison, Malcolm asked for "forgiveness for the unkind things I said in the past." After experiencing the "graciousness" of Muslims "of all colors" on his pilgrimage to Mecca, Malcolm no longer believed that whites were devils. His goal now was to unite all African American organizations to achieve equality.[11] Rosa Parks met Malcolm X after his pilgrimage and just one week before his assassination. Parks recalled, "I had a lot of admiration for him, considering his background and where he came from and his having had to struggle so hard just to reach the point of being respected as a leader of the Black

Malcolm X attending court in Queens, NY, in 1964. Photograph by Herman Hiller. (Library of Congress)

Muslims." According to historian Douglas Brinkley, Parks read everything she could find about Malcolm X, his establishment of a Muslim
mosque in Harlem, and the Organization of Afro-American Unity.[12]
Parks sat in the front row at a speech Malcolm gave in Detroit. She
recalled, "I spoke to him and he autographed the program for me."[13]
The next Sunday, February 21, 1965, as he was about to speak at a rally
at the Audubon Ballroom, in Harlem, three members of the Nation of
Islam shot and killed him.

The two major social problems of the 1960s were racism and poverty. By the mid-1960s, the civil rights movement had made impressive
legislative gains to alleviate racism—*Brown v. Board of Education*, the
Civil Rights Act of 1964, the Voting Rights Act of 1965, and the 24th
Amendment outlawing the poll tax had all become law. The federal
government had taken a compelling stand in support of equality for all
Americans. Although white racists still resisted desegregation in some
parts of the South, in many areas racial integration was proceeding. Despite the gains African Americans saw in the southern states, blacks in
the urban north were making less progress. The civil rights movement
raised the expectations of northern blacks, but the movement was unable to address their difficult economic concerns. "White flight" had
decimated the inner cities, eroding the tax base, leaving less money for
city services, and eliminating good jobs for city residents. The urban
population was getting poorer; taxes were increasing, and costs of food
and housing rose. In 1962, Michael Harrington's *The Other America*
exposed the problem of poverty in America, and in 1964, President
Lyndon Johnson introduced his War on Poverty to mitigate the worst
effects of poverty in America. But poverty could not be legislated away.
The underlying structural problems—such as unemployment, poor
housing, and inadequate education—were difficult to resolve.

The outbreak of urban riots in northern cities focused the nation's
attention on the racial and economic inequalities African Americans
were facing across the United States. In the summers of 1965, 1966,
and 1967, urban rioters burned and looted parts of cities from Los Angeles, California, to Detroit, Michigan, and Newark, New Jersey. The
riots came as a surprise to people in the White House, the Department
of Justice, and the Federal Bureau of Investigation—no one expected
the "race problem" to explode in the north. In the end, the estimates
of property damages from the riots ran into the millions and nearly one

hundred people, mostly African Americans, died. In the summer of 1967, President Johnson established a National Advisory Commission on Civil Disorders, commonly known as the Kerner Commission, to answer three questions: What happened? Why did it happen? What can be done to prevent it from happening again?[14] After a year of investigating conditions of employment, education, the welfare system, and housing, the commission concluded its report with the following statement:

> We have uncovered no startling truths, no unique insights, no simple solutions. The destruction and the bitterness of racial disorder, the harsh polemics of black revolt and white repression have been seen and heard before in this country. It is time now to end the destruction and the violence, not only in the streets of the ghetto but in the lives of people.[15]

"Our nation," the commission reported, "is moving toward two societies, one black, one white—separate and unequal."[16] The Kerner Commission report made a series of modest proposals for change, but local, state, and federal governments implemented few of the programs.

For Rosa Parks, the Detroit riot of July 23, 1967, was appalling. Despite Parks's personal reservations about nonviolence, she did not condone irrational violent acts, and to her, the Detroit riot was just that—a series of irrational violent acts. The trouble began when police raided an after-hours drinking club, a "blind pig," located at 12th Street, an area described in news reports as a "dirty street of small stores, pawn shops, bars and clothing stores...a street of crime and prostitution." Police arrested 73 people.[17] After the arrests, a mob formed near the club; they accused the police of brutality and began throwing bottles and cans at them. Soon things escalated into looting and arson. By Monday morning, uncontrolled violence had spread throughout the city. Thousands of African Americans took part; the police arrested 600 adults and 100 juveniles. Mayor Jesse Cavanagh contacted Governor George Romney for help when 700 national guardsmen, 200 state police troopers, and 600 Detroit police officers failed to quell the riot. The governor ordered 800 additional national guardsmen with tanks into Detroit, imposed a curfew from 9 P.M. to 5:30 A.M., halted the sale of alcoholic beverages, and closed the schools and parks, all to no avail. Looters ransacked a four-mile section of Woodward Avenue; looting and firebombs destroyed a three-mile section of Grand River and raged along 18 blocks of 12th Street. Flames consumed much of a 20-block section of Grand River; block-long sections of tenements and small businesses were destroyed. When unruly mobs threw bricks, bottles, and other debris at firefighters, many of the latter decided to end their efforts to save the flaming buildings and pulled back. Later black residents of the most severely impacted areas, armed with rifles, positioned themselves around the firefighters, protecting them from the mobs. When the riot finally ended on July 30, 1967, some 5,000 people were homeless, police had arrested more than 7,000, the total number of people seriously injured topped 700, and 43 people were dead.[18] Dennis Archer, a former Detroit mayor, remembered, "about 1,300 buildings, homes or businesses, where people don't even shop today, were destroyed."[19] The riot affected Rosa Parks personally as well. According to historian Douglas Brinkley, looters destroyed Raymond Parks's small barbershop, stealing all of his haircutting tools; rioters vandalized the Parks's new car; and protesters beat some of their friends during the mayhem. Parks recalled that her apartment was just a half block from where the rioting was going on. When Raymond ventured outside after the governor imposed a curfew, the national guardsmen threatened him. Raymond, she recalled was very upset by what was going on; he could not eat or sleep. Eventually his doctor prescribed a sedative to quiet his nerves.[20] The riot, according to Parks, was "pure hooliganism" perpetrated by "thieves," but she also recognized that frustration and deprivation played a role. Yet Parks believed that the civil rights movement was irrevocably hurt when blacks passed off looting and burning as civil rights activism,[21] and she denounced the mobs.

The 1960s were a turbulent time in America, and 1968 was the worst year of the decade. In January 1968, the United States suffered a crippling psychological defeat in Vietnam when the North Vietnamese launched a surprise offensive, attacking almost every major city in South Vietnam during Têt, the Vietnamese New Year. In a televised report on Vietnam in February, journalist Walter Cronkite concluded with a personal commentary in which he voiced his strong belief that the war would end in stalemate. Then on March 31, 1968, President

Lyndon Johnson stunned the nation when he announced, "I shall not seek, and I will not accept, the nomination of my party for another term as your President."[22] It seemed as if the United States were coming apart at the seams, but the worst was yet to come.

On April 3, Martin Luther King, Jr., traveled to Memphis, Tennessee, to lead a campaign for sanitation workers protesting their low wages and poor working conditions. According to historian Michael Honey, King was trying to form a coalition linking labor and civil rights. "He called for a general strike in the city of Memphis by workers, domestic workers, teachers, students," Honey said. "And this would have been a tremendous high point in the civil rights movement. Nothing like this had happened in any city. It would also be a tremendous high point in the labor movement."[23] That evening, King delivered a speech to a relatively small crowd that had gathered to hear him speak despite bad weather. In concluding the sermon, King said,

> Like anybody, I would like to live a long life. Longevity has its place. But I'm not concerned about that now. I just want to do God's will. And He's allowed me to go up to the mountain. And I've looked over. And I've seen the Promised Land. I may not get there with you. But I want you to know tonight, that we, as a people, will get to the promised land![24]

On April 4, 1968, as he was standing on the balcony of the Lorraine Motel, Martin Luther King, Jr., was shot in the neck. He died a short time later at the hospital. King's assassination sparked another round of urban riots in more than a hundred cities nationwide. On April 9, tens of thousands of people lined the streets of Atlanta, Georgia, to pay tribute to King as his casket passed by in a wooden cart drawn by a single mule.

Rosa Parks and her mother were listening to the radio on April 4. She remembered that they had expected to hear King deliver a sermon, since his sermons usually were broadcast during Lent. Instead they heard another minister speaking. His sermon was broken off by the announcement that King had been shot. The news soon followed that King had died. Parks said, "I was deeply grieved. Mama and I wept quietly together."[25]

After King's assassination, Sheldon Tappes, a local UAW labor leader in Detroit, made arrangements for Rosa Parks and his wife, Louise Tappes, and several others in Detroit to travel to Memphis to continue the march that King had been leading. According to historian Douglas Brinkley, when Parks got to Memphis, she spoke with many of the striking sanitation workers, but they, too, were in despair. No one wanted to continue the demonstration in Memphis, nevertheless, the next day Coretta Scott King continued her husband's work in Memphis. Singer Harry Belafonte was in Memphis as well, and after a few hours offered to take Parks to Atlanta in his private plane for King's funeral. At the funeral, Parks met Democratic presidential candidate Robert F. Kennedy and his wife, Ethel. According to Parks, a few weeks later she had a dream about King rising up the chimney of a large fireplace. "And facing him, with his back toward me, was a young white man with dark hair and a small build."[26] Parks later interpreted her dream as a premonition because two months later, on June 5, 1968, Sirhan Sirhan, a lone gunman, assassinated Senator Robert Kennedy in the ballroom of the Ambassador Hotel in Los Angeles.[27] For many African Americans, Kennedy's death was as devastating as King's death had been. Kennedy, too, was committed to the rights of African Americans to vote, receive an equal education, and use public accommodations. In her autobiography, Parks recorded her discouragement in the face of loss after loss.[28]

The civil rights era was ending, and Parks along with other African Americans mourned the loss. However, the movement achieved impressive judicial and legislative victories; Parks and the thousands of other activists had changed America forever. *Brown v. Board of Education* not only prohibited segregated public schools, it overturned the 1896 *Plessy v. Ferguson* decision supporting legal segregation. The Civil Rights Act of 1964 ushered in significant changes. It banned the unequal application of voter registration requirements and outlawed discrimination in all places of public accommodations engaged in interstate commerce. It authorized the U.S. attorney general to file suits to force school desegregation and permitted the federal government to withdraw funds from programs that practiced discrimination. It outlawed discrimination in employment in any business employing 25 people or more and created an Equal Employment Opportunity Commission to review complaints.[29] The Voting Rights Act went further than any legislation before to strengthen voting rights for African Americans. The act enabled the attorney general to "appoint federal examiners to supervise voter registration in states or voting districts where literacy or other qualifying tests were in use and where fewer than 50 percent of voting age residents were registered or had voted in 1964."[30] The 24th Amendment eliminated the poll tax. Rosa Parks knew these were important changes, but more needed to be accomplished and young people would have to carry on the struggle.

NOTES

1. Nonviolent Resistance, http://mlk-kpp01.stanford.edu/index.php/encyclopedia/encyclopedia/enc_nonviolent_resistance/ (accessed August 25, 2009).

2. Rosa Parks with Jim Haskins, *My Story* (New York: Penguin Books, 1992), 178.

3. Jannell McGrew, "Close Friend, Activist Has Special Perspective," *Montgomery Advertiser* (April 6, 2009).

4. Amy Goodman, "John Conyers on Rosa Parks: 'She Earned the Title as Mother of the Civil Rights Movement,'" Democracy Now, http://www.democracynow.org/2005/10/25/john_conyers_on_rosa_parks_she (accessed August 25, 2009).

5. Douglas Brinkley, *Rosa Parks; A Life* (New York: Penguin Books, 2000), 189.

6. Parks, *My Story*, 174–75.

7. Donald Jansen, "Muslims Press Race Separation," *New York Times*, February 26, 1963, 3.

8. Ibid.

9. Bob Garfield, An Interview with Timothy Tyson, "Tabula Rosa," http://www.onthemedia.org/transcripts/2009/07/03/02 (accessed August 25, 2009).

10. "X Marks the Spot," *Newsweek* (May 6, 1963): 28.

11. "Malcolm X Woos 2 Rights Leaders," *New York Times*, May 19, 1964, 28.

12. Parks, *My Story*, 177–78; Brinkley, *Rosa Parks*, 192.

13. Parks, *My Story*, 177.

14. *Report of the National Advisory Commission on Civil Disorders*, http://www.eisenhowerfoundation.org/docs/kerner.pdf (accessed August 26, 2009).

15. Ibid.

16. Ibid.

17. "Detroit Is Swept by Rioting and Fires; Romney Calls in Guard; 700 Arrested," *New York Times*, July 24, 1967, 1.

18. Ibid.

19. Mayhem in the City: The Detroit Riots, http://www.npr.org/templates/story/story.php?storyId=12195165 (accessed August 26, 2009).

20. Marcia M. Greenlee, "Interview with Rosa McCauley Parks" on August 22 and 23, 1978, in *The Black Woman Oral History Project*, vol. 8, ed. Ruth Edmonds Hill (Westport, CT: Meckler, 1991), 256–57.

21. Brinkley, *Rosa Parks*, 203; Greenlee, "Interview with Rosa McCauley Parks," 256.

22. President Lyndon B. Johnson's Address to the Nation, March 31, 1968, http://www.lbjlib.utexas.edu/Johnson/archives.hom/speeches.hom/680331.asp (accessed August 26, 2009).

23. Chris Simkins, "Martin Luther King, Jr., Remembered on 40th Anniversary of Assassination," http://www.voanews.com/english/archive/2008–04/2008–04–03-voa29.cfm?moddate=2008–04–03 (accessed August 26, 2009).

24. "I've Been to the Mountaintop," Martin Luther King Papers, http://mlk-kpp01.stanford.edu/index.php/kingpapers/article/a_call_to_conscience_the_landmark_speeches_of_martin_luther_king_jr_content/ (accessed August 26, 2009).

25. Parks, *My Story*, 179.

26. Parks, *My Story*, 179–80; Brinkley, *Rosa Parks*, 205–6.

27. Robert F. Kennedy Assassination (Summary), http://foia.fbi.gov/foiaindex/rfkasumm.htm (accessed August 27, 2009).

28. Parks, *My Story*, 180.

29. Major Features of the Civil Rights Act of 1964, http://www.congresslink.org/print_basics_histmats_civilrights64text.htm (accessed August 27, 2009).

30. Voting Rights Act of 1965, http://www.congresslink.org/print_basics_histmats_votingrights_contents.htm (accessed August 27, 2009).

Chapter 9

AFTER THE CIVIL RIGHTS MOVEMENT

The 1970s were a time of great personal loss for Rosa Parks. Doctors had diagnosed Raymond with throat cancer, and in August 1977 Raymond Parks died at the age of 74. Raymond's death was a devastating blow to Rosa Parks. According to historian Douglas Brinkley, Raymond had never been financially successful, but he was a loyal husband and a source of strength to Rosa Parks. Raymond never tried to stop his wife from attending civil rights demonstrations or traveling to conferences or workshops. "He respected her, and for that she loved him unconditionally," Brinkley wrote.[1] In November of the same year, Parks's brother Sylvester passed away from stomach cancer. Her mother, Leona, was also fighting cancer. Parks recalled traveling to three separate hospitals every day to see her husband, her brother, and her mother in turn. After Raymond's death and at the onset of Leona's cancer, Parks was unable to care for her mother and still keep her job, so she placed Leona in a nursing home for a year. Nevertheless, she visited her mother every day, at every meal.[2] The stress of losing both her husband and brother, working, and being at the nursing home three times a day, seven days a week, was overwhelming for Parks. She, too, was having health problems. The ulcers she developed while in Montgomery grew worse, and she began having heart problems. At this point Parks decided that the best solution was for her to move into a senior citizen apartment building. Parks then moved Leona out of the nursing home and into the apartment, where Parks cared for her until Leona passed away in 1979 at the age of 91.[3] For the first time in her life, Rosa Parks was alone.

Not only did Parks lose her family, she was losing her place in the movement that she had helped to launch when she refused to move from her seat on the Cleveland Avenue bus on December 1, 1955. The movement grounded in Martin Luther King's vision of nonviolence was dying. Without King's charismatic leadership, the SCLC became irrelevant, while internal battles over principles and beliefs tore the NAACP and SNCC apart. The new generation of young activists had a new rallying cry: "black power." New leaders such as Stokley Carmichael, Huey Newton, and Bobby Seale no longer called on protestors to "turn the other cheek" or "receive brutality with love." According to this new generation, African Americans had won the right to vote, to enroll in a white school, to sit at a white lunch counter or in the front of a bus, but most black Americans still lived in poverty. True social change, many argued, could not come with integration. They called for revolution, and by the late 1960s, they became the dominant voice of young black America.

Historian Douglas Brinkley wrote that during the 1970s, "Parks's image became more symbolic and less activist...no one seemed to care anymore how she viewed the state of American society."[4] Perhaps that was outwardly true, but it really did not differ from the way most people treated Rosa Parks throughout her life. Even in Montgomery in 1955, the ministers became the public voice of the boycott; after they introduced Parks at the mass meeting at the Holt Street Baptist Church, she asked if she should say anything. They told her, "You have had enough and you have said enough and you don't have to speak."[5] They did not ask Parks to speak, nor did they ask her to speak at any subsequent mass meetings. No one came forward to ask what she thought about the state of American society then, and no one asked her later. Nevertheless, Rosa Parks was a political activist then and she remained a political activist later, although not within the traditionally defined meaning of politics. For Parks, Ella Baker, Septima Clark, and many other women activists, politics meant any "activity [that] includes all community work which is oriented to change through multifaceted goals including service, support, public education and advocacy."[6] Rosa Parks did not run for office and she did not hold office, but she remained a political activist who continued to be keenly interested in issues of social justice. She had an earnest interest in local political issues and elections, continued to work in John Conyers's office, and remained active in the NAACP.

Others, however, were content to see Parks as simply an icon, a piece of history; and they treated her as such. In 1975, Montgomery commemorated the 1955 bus boycott with a weekend program they called The Struggle Continues. In three days of conferences, participants called on African Americans to become more involved in "the nation's politics, economics, and education while calling for full employment and a Congressional investigation into the assassination of Rev. Dr. Martin Luther King, Jr., the civil rights leader who came to prominence in the boycott." Montgomery's Mayor Jim Robinson, Representative John Conyers, Representative Andrew Young, and Leon Hall, the conference organizer, all spoke about the gains African Americans had made since the boycott, cataloging the number of black police officers, councilmen, and state officeholders in place. The conference organizers apparently did not ask Rosa Parks to reflect on the political, economic, or social progress of African Americans since the boycott. Reporters wrote that Parks merely "summed up her action of 20 years ago." Everyone simply wanted Parks to reiterate the reasons she decided not to give up her seat. The newspaper quoted Parks as saying she "only wanted to be a citizen—to be treated like a citizen." She concluded her remarks by telling the crowd, "Don't stop. Keep on. Keep on keeping on."[7] The world made Rosa Parks a symbol, a martyr, a saint. No one asked her what she thought, no one asked her what strategies she believed African Americans should use to move forward, no one wanted to see her as she really was—a strong, determined, political activist.

This fictional Rosa Parks, the iconic image the world had created, was bolstered over the years through the myriad awards and honors bestowed upon her. In 1971, the NAACP awarded Parks its Roy Wilkins Award in honor her efforts to make a difference at the annual Fight for Freedom Dinner. Each year the NAACP awards its Spingarn Medal, named for J. E. Spingarn, an early member and second president of the NAACP, to a person of "African descent and American citizenship who shall have made the highest achievement during the preceding year or years in any honorable field of human endeavor." In 1957, the NAACP presented the award to Martin Luther King, Jr., not Rosa Parks, "for leadership role in the Montgomery bus protest movement." Between 1958 and 1978, 21 recipients—including Daisy Bates and the Little Rock Nine, Duke Ellington, Langston Hughes, Medgar Evers, Sammy Davis, Jr., and Hank Aaron—received the award. It would take 24 years after the boycott for the organization Rosa Parks had supported since 1943 to recognize her role in launching the modern civil rights movement. In 1979, the NAACP awarded Parks the Spingarn Medal "In recognition to the quiet courage and determination exemplified when she refused to surrender her seat on a Montgomery, Alabama bus."[8] As far as the NAACP was concerned, Rosa Parks was frozen in time.

Perhaps no award or honor highlights the degree to which people misunderstood Rosa Parks better than the presentation of the Martin Luther King, Jr., Nonviolent Peace Prize in 1980. The King Center awards this prize

> for commitment to nonviolence as a way of life, recognizes achievements in the eradication of poverty, and racism and the successful quest for alternatives to war. The award highlights individuals who use nonviolent strategies to gain social justice, human rights, and civil rights liberties.[9]

Once again, Parks received an award based solely on her nonviolent actions during her arrest on December 1, 1955. Obviously, no one had bothered to ask her about her views on nonviolence as a way of life since by then she had abandoned those views. Receiving this award again reinforced the image of Rosa Parks as a one-dimensional iconic figure.

Despite her public image, Rosa Parks continued her political activism. In addition to being honored at tribute dinners and receiving awards, Parks began working with young people. She accepted a significant number of invitations to speak to schoolchildren and became the honorary secretary of the Afrikan History Club, a McFarlane Elementary

School club. Parks visited the club, spoke to the children about black history, and attended club plays. She also participated in the Edmundson Community School Program, teaching adult sewing classes.[10]

In 1975, Parks became a member of the Joan Little Defense Committee. A grand jury had indicted Joan Little, a 20-year-old black woman, for first-degree murder in Washington, North Carolina. Previously, a jury had convicted Little of breaking and entering. As Little sat in jail awaiting an appeal hearing on her conviction, Clarence Alligood, a 62-year-old white deputy, came to her cell in search of sex three times between 10 P.M. on August 26 and 3 A.M. on August 27.

> Rebuffed the first time, he returned with a present of cigarettes and sandwiches. He left, but soon came back. "By then," she testified, "I had changed into my nightgown. He was telling me I really looked nice in my gown, and he wanted to have sex with me." Alligood pulled off his trousers and shoes in the hall and entered her cell with a grin. "He said he had been nice to me, and it was time I was nice to him. I told him I didn't feel like I should be nice to him that way." Her voice becoming almost inaudible, she testified that Alligood fondled her, then removed her nightgown. "That's when I noticed he had the ice pick in his hand."[11]

Little resisted, grabbed the ice pick, stabbed Alligood, and fled. She turned herself in to police after she learned that Alligood was dead. Police charged Joan Little with murder in the first degree. Attorneys volunteered to represent Little pro bono and then submitted a motion to have the court assume the costs of expert witnesses because Little was indigent. The judge denied the motion. When Little's story became national news, Detroit Councilwoman Erma Henderson and Dean Henry Fagin of the University of Detroit began a campaign to raise funds for Little's trial expenses. Georgia Congressman Julian Bond headed the nationwide campaign, and Rosa Parks served on the committee in Detroit. Parks was one of four volunteers who wrote 3,000 letters asking for donations to churches, women's groups, and college fraternities and sororities.[12] Jurors found Joan Little not guilty.

In addition to working with children and working with the Joan Little Defense Fund, Rosa Parks was a member of numerous local groups working to improve conditions in Detroit. In 1972, she became a member of the United Community Services Black Caucus, and a year later joined the United Community Services of Metropolitan Detroit, an organization concerned with the impact of the federal budget on services in Detroit, including mental health, hospital care, and housing. As a part of the political Urban Alliance, Parks worked with others to recommend candidates for the school board. Finally, Parks worked with her neighborhood block club to clean up the neighborhood, welcome new neighbors, advocate voter registration, work with parents and children, and promote awareness of current issues.[13]

Rosa Parks's public persona may have been that of a symbol—an icon. And many of the awards she received in her lifetime reinforced that notion. In reality, Parks remained politically active and engaged. She worked to improve the quality of life for African Americans in Detroit and elsewhere. Women like Rosa Parks entered the public arena and fought for essential reforms while grounded in networks of kin, church, and community.[14] To dismiss this work as apolitical, to declare that Parks became a symbol and less an activist, is a fundamental misreading of history.

After her husband, brother, and mother passed away, Rosa Parks's relationship with Elaine Eason Steele began to change. Parks and Steele originally became friends in 1964 when they both worked at the Stockton Sewing Company. According to historian Douglas Brinkley, Steele became "for all intents and purposes, the daughter Rosa Parks never had as well as her best friend and personal manager." Brinkley, who interviewed Steele, wrote that in 1968, Steele was a radical black activist, a member of the Republic of New Africa, a group that was advocating a separate black state be set aside within the United States. Brinkley asserts that by spending time with Parks, Steele's radicalism diminished, and by 1972, Steele embraced Christian Universalism. "I learned through Mrs. Parks," said Steele, "not to have animosity or hate or be judgmental." While Parks worked in John Conyers's office, Steele worked in the offices of the U.S. District Court. Parks and Steele carpooled together and became quite close. According to Brinkley, they worked together on community and civil rights activities.[15]

As their relationship deepened, Steele "made herself an iron drawbridge between Parks and journalists or any other visitor who wanted a word with the aging icon." Steele began scheduling and accompanying Parks when she made public appearances. She wanted to make sure no one took advantage of Parks's "sweet spirit." Rosa Parks's nieces and nephews, however, had a very different opinion. They accused Steele of using Parks, of marketing her role in the bus boycott for money. Steele denied the allegations, claiming that she was protecting Parks from bankruptcy and exhaustion.[16] Steele argued that she protected Parks from camera-toting tourists and school children. She no longer allowed people who stopped by Conyers's office to snap photos of Parks. When Parks was involved in an automobile accident in 1987, Steele kept reporters away. After Parks underwent surgery to have a pacemaker installed in 1988, Steele made the decision to cancel almost all of Parks's speaking engagements. Steele also arranged for Parks to spend her winters in Los Angeles. In 1989, Parks's closest friend, Louise Tappes, died, and Steele's role in Parks's life expanded. Rosa Parks was rarely seen at award ceremonies, dinners, or accepting honorary degrees without Steele at her side.[17]

In 1987 Rosa Parks and Elaine Eason Steele created the Rosa and Raymond Parks Institute for Self-Development, an after-school program that taught children "quiet strength" and self-paced study. Although Rosa and Raymond Parks had no children of their own, Rosa always enjoyed working with young people. In Montgomery, Parks served as the adviser of the NAACP Youth Council, inspiring and motivating children to achieve their highest potential and teaching them never to lose their dignity. Claudette Colvin remembered that "Mrs. Parks said always do what is right." Rosa Parks worked with children in Detroit as well, visiting schools, supporting black history programs, and attending events. The mission of the institute was to teach 11- to 17-year-old underprivileged children "how to conduct themselves with dignity and honor in the modern world."[18] "Too many young people are not staying in school and taking advantage of the opportunities they have," Parks told *Ebony*. "They're not motivated to learn what is necessary to get the good positions, the good jobs, to go into business for themselves."[19] In 1997 Parks submitted a proposal to the Detroit Board of Education to establish a charter school, the Rosa and Raymond Parks Academy for Self-Development, one of 12 proposals submitted that year,[20] but apparently, the board rejected Parks's application. Nevertheless, Parks

continued working with students, modeling her program on other successful programs in the area.

In 1989, the Michigan Coalition for Human Rights (MCHR) began
a program that took buses full of students from the Detroit area to famous civil rights sites in the South. MCHR believed that these tours
would teach young people about the history of racism and help them
understand the civil rights movement by visiting and learning about
historic landmarks. Organizers hoped that the program would develop
a new generation of young leaders committed to working for racial justice in their communities and around the world.[21] Parks and Steele
modeled their own program on the MCHR program. The institute's
Pathways to Freedom program "traces the physical and philosophical
path of the civil rights movement" for about 150 young people each
summer. According to Executive Director Anita Peek,

> Although not all institute participants join the summer Pathways
> to Freedom trip, institute classes are considered preparation for
> the ride. Programs are positive, emphasizing substance abuse pre-
> vention, etiquette, nutrition, banking skills, life skills and reading
> comprehension. Another program enlists young people to teach
> computer skills to senior citizens.[22]

Every year the Pathways to Freedom program selects a different historical place for students to conduct field research. Previous programs
have included traveling to the Great Plains to learn about Buffalo Soldiers, to Oklahoma to study the Trail of Tears, to Harper's Ferry to learn
about John Brown, and to Nova Scotia to begin an extended study of
the Underground Railroad. The summer programs are quite popular.
Students from around the country enroll in the month-long program,
despite prohibitions on television, radio, and video games. Participants
keep a journal of the trip and present oral reports on what they have
learned. Between 1987 and 2000, when Parks went on the tour, more
than five thousand students took part in the program. At that time
Parks also spoke to the students about personal responsibility during
the tour. "I'm hoping that we'll reach as many young people as we can
and that they will be motivated, trained, and inspired to reach their
highest potential in life," Parks said.[23]

Today the institute continues to offer its Pathways to Freedom summer program, supported by extended curriculum work in Pathways chapters in seven states as well as the Bahamas and Canada. In addition, learning centers in Michigan and California offer classes for senior citizens in basic computer literacy, which are taught by young people. After the attack on the World Trade Center in New York on September 11, 2001, the Rosa Parks Institute initiated a collaborative program with the Boggs Center for Community Leadership and Wayne State University's Multicultural Experience in Leadership Development Program to promote understanding and healing among young people. The program designed a Youth Peace Summit series that reviewed how the media influenced peace and connected the young people to the global community through a United Nations Youth Assembly.[24]

Rosa Parks was in the news again on August 31, 1994, having spent the night under police protection after an unknown assailant robbed her of $53 and assaulted her in her home. About 8 P.M. on August 30, Parks told the police she was upstairs when she heard noises downstairs.

On September 27, 1994, Judge Richard Halloran of Detroit's 36th District Court swore in Rosa Parks before her testimony concerning the events of August 30, 1994, when she was assaulted and robbed at her Detroit home. (AP Photo/Richard Sheinwald)

When she went downstairs to investigate, she found a man reeking of alcohol in her home. The back door was broken off the hinges, and the man told her he had chased off an intruder. Then he hit her. He told Parks that he wanted money. "When she went upstairs to get some cash, he followed, demanded more money and began to strike her, she said. He said, 'If you don't give me more then I'm going to have to hurt you,'" Parks said. The man left immediately after Parks gave him the money. According to news reports, Parks suffered bruises to her face and chest. A few days later, *New York Times* writer Bob Herbert reported that Parks said, "I had never been hit in that manner in my life. I was screaming and trying to ask him not to hit me.... In these times," she continued, "none of us seems to be safe from this type of treatment and violation by a sick-minded person...we still have a long way to go, and so many children are going astray."[25] On August 31, police arrested Joseph Skipper at a local grocery store when customers recognized him from a composite sketch and called police. Americans and people around the world condemned the assault and the assailant. Annette Pointer, a neighbor said, "Who in their sick mind would bother an 81-year-old woman who has been an asset to the community all of her life? I cannot believe it." Horace Sheffield, who participated in civil rights demonstrations in Montgomery with Parks, said: "Anyone who could attack her is beyond the pale. This is senseless."[26] Editorials in newspapers across the country denounced the assault. The incident prompted Parks to move away from downtown Detroit. Parks's move to the Riverfront Towers, a gated and guarded high-rise building, widened the rift between her family and Elaine Eason Steele. According to her nieces and nephews, they were becoming increasingly concerned about their aunt's "hectic schedule and her dependence on Steele." Her family claimed that after the move, it became difficult for them to arrange visits with their beloved aunt.[27]

Rosa Parks's schedule did, in fact, seem hectic. She continued to make appearances across the country in support of civil rights and voter registration and received countless awards for her part in the Montgomery Bus Boycott. In 1990, the New York State African American Political Action Committee awarded Parks the Adam Clayton Powell, Jr., Legislative Achievement Award for her "impact on the quality of life for African Americans." In 1991, a bronze sculpture of Parks went on display at the National Portrait Gallery in Washington, D.C. In 1994, the organizers of One Day of Peace, a Swedish festival, announced that they had created the Rosa Parks Peace Prize. Donations from Swedish corporations and citizens endowed the prize. In 1996, Rosa Parks was one of 11 recipients of the Medal of Freedom, awarded by President Bill Clinton, for her role in sparking the civil rights movement. In 1998, Parks participated in Jesse Jackson's "Save the Dream" march in Los Angeles, and she addressed the Million Man March held in Washington, D.C. That same year, Parks was photographed with Spike Lee and Dustin Hoffman at the Academy Awards.[28]

Perhaps the greatest honor Rosa Parks received was the 121st Congressional Gold Medal, the highest award bestowed by the U.S. government, in June 1999. Representative Julia Carson (D-Indiana) and Senator Spencer Abraham (R-Michigan) introduced the bill to honor Parks with the Congressional Award, it passed both houses of Congress

President Bill Clinton awarded Rosa Parks the Presidential Medal of Freedom in the Oval Office on September 14, 1996. (AP Photo/Joe Marquette)

by wide margins, and President Clinton signed it into law. An audience of 650 attended the ceremony in Washington, including many civil rights activists. In his remarks, President Clinton said, "In so many ways Rosa Parks brought America home to our founders' dream. We must never ever, when this ceremony is over, forget about the power of ordinary people to stand in the fire for the cause of human dignity."[29]

In December 2000, Troy State University in Montgomery dedicated a $10-million university library and interactive museum named for Rosa Parks, located at the site of her 1955 arrest. From her wheelchair, Parks waved to the audience of about a thousand who attended the event. At the same ceremony, Alabama governor Donald Siegelman awarded Parks the first Governor's Medal of Honor for Extraordinary Courage, and Mayor Bobby Bright proclaimed December 1 Rosa Parks Day. The Rosa Parks Library and Museum included a statue of Parks, an exhibit recounting her conversation with James Blake, the bus driver, and an old bus that was used in Montgomery in 1955. By 2002, the National Park Service had put Rosa Parks's apartment on Cleveland Avenue on the National Register of Historic Places.[30] Even the bus on which Rosa Parks was arrested had become an historic treasure. After the bus sat in an Alabama field for more than thirty years, Henry Ford Museum conservator Malcolm Collum examined the vehicle and consulted with various experts about its restoration. In September 2002, the President's Committee on the Arts and Humanities announced that the Rosa Parks bus project had received $205,000 in funding through the Save America's Treasures Program for the restoration project. The Henry Ford Museum placed the Rosa Parks bus on exhibit on February 1, 2003.[31]

Rosa Parks's health was continuing to deteriorate. In 1998, Steele found her lying unconscious at home. An ambulance rushed Parks to the hospital and she pulled through, but from then on, she needed a walker or wheelchair to get around. Her family continued to worry. Rhea McCauley, one of Parks's nieces, unsuccessfully petitioned a court to become Parks's guardian. According to McCauley, that was the last time she saw her aunt, who was by then frail and tearful. To the family, Rosa Parks was not a celebrity or an icon, she was a "beloved aunt who delighted in their huge annual family reunions, who was always reading and inquiring about current affairs, always willing to look at life in a fresh way. In her 80s," they recalled, "she became a vegetarian, took up yoga, and learned the computer."[32]

They became even more concerned when Parks's name appeared on a $5 billion lawsuit against the Atlanta-based rap duo OutKast. Out-Kast's 1998 album, *Aquemini*, included a hit song entitled "Rosa Parks," and although she was not mentioned in the lyrics, the chorus included the words, "Ah ha, hush that fuss/ Everybody move to the back of the bus." The lawsuit claimed that OutKast "commercially exploited" Parks and damaged her reputation by using her name on the record. According to her lawyers, Parks wanted her name removed from the record in the future, in addition to seeking unspecified monetary damages. A federal court judge dismissed OutKast from the suit, and Parks's lawyers filed a second suit in August 2004, naming BMG, Arista Records LLC, and LaFace Records. They sought more than $5 billion in damages. In December 2003, the U.S. Supreme Court ruled that the case could proceed.[33]

Meanwhile, Rosa Parks's family was becoming more and more concerned. In 2004, at the age of 91, Parks was diagnosed with dementia. She was incapable of explaining why she had decided to sue OutKast and their record company. Parks's nieces and nephews argued that their Aunt Rosa, who had lived a humble, frugal life, would never have sued for money. They accused her lawyer, Gregory Reed, and Elaine Eason Steele of exploiting Parks for private gain. Reed denied the allegations, saying, "It would be a greater damage to her legacy not to bring that suit." Steele declined to comment.[34] In 2004 U.S. District Judge George Steeh appointed Dennis Archer a former Michigan Supreme Court justice, past president of the American Bar Association, and former Detroit mayor as temporary independent guardian for Parks. Archer reviewed all litigation files to determine if Parks was being represented fairly in the lawsuit.[35] In May 2005, Rosa Parks, OutKast, and Sony BMG Music Entertainment came to an out-of-court settlement. The defendants admitted no wrongdoing but agreed to work on projects "to enlighten today's youth about the significant role Rosa Parks played in making America a better place for all races."[36]

Rosa Parks passed away on October 24, 2005, at age 92, in her Detroit home, of natural causes.[37] Her obituary appeared in media outlets around the world, each one chronicling the events of December 1, 1955, and the subsequent Montgomery Bus Boycott in great detail. Many of the newspapers, weekly magazines, radio, and television reports highlighted Parks's many honors and awards; some even mentioned the

Raymond and Rosa Parks Institute for Self-Development. None told about Parks's political activism after the bus boycott. Rosa Parks would remain a symbol—an American icon frozen in time.

NOTES

1. Douglas Brinkley, *Rosa Parks; A Life* (New York: Penguin Books, 2000), 210.

2. Rosa Parks with Jim Haskins, *My Story* (New York: Penguin Books, 1992), 180.

3. Ibid., 180–81; Brinkley, *Rosa Parks*, 209.

4. Brinkley, *Rosa Parks*, 207.

5. Parks, *My Story*, 139.

6. Linda Christiansen-Ruffman, "Women's Conceptions of the Political: Theoretical Contributions to a Study of Women's Organizations," in *Feminist Organizations: Harvest of the New Women's Movement*, ed. Myra Marx Ferree and Patricia Yancy (Newbury Park, CA: Sage Publications, 1987).

7. Thomas A. Johnson, "'55 Montgomery Bus Boycott Marked," *New York Times*, December 8, 1975.

8. "The Spingard Medal," http://www.naacp.org/events/spingarn/index.htm (accessed August 28, 2009).

9. The King Center, "Commemorative Service," http://www.the kingcenter.org/KingHoliday/Commemorative.aspx (accessed August 28, 2009).

10. Rosa L. Parks Papers, Walter Reuther Archives of Labor and Urban Affairs, box 1, folder 3; box 2, folder 3.

11. "Trials: Joan Little's Story," *Time* magazine, http://www.time.com/time/magazine/article/0,9171,913413,00.html (accessed August 28, 2009).

12. Angela Davis, "Joan Little: The Dialectics of Rape," *Ms. Magazine* http://www.msmagazine.com/spring2002/davis.asp (accessed August 28, 2009); Rosa L. Parks Papers, Walter Reuther Archives of Labor and Urban Affairs, box 3, folder 1.

13. Rosa L. Parks Papers, Walter Reuther Archives of Labor and Urban Affairs, box 3, folder 11.

14. Martha Ackelsberg and Irene Diamond, "Gender and Political Life," in *Analyzing Gender: A Handbook of Social Science Research*, ed.

Beth B. Hess and Myra Marx Ferree (Beverly Hills, CA: Sage Publications, 1987), 509, 518–19.

15. Brinkley, *Rosa Parks*, 211.

16. Ibid., 212.

17. Ibid., 213.

18. Ibid.

19. "Rosa MCauley," *Africana Studies*, Department of Africana Studies at Stony Brook University, Stony Brook, NY, http://www.sunysb.edu/afs/?afsphotos/rparks (accessed August 28, 2009).

20. Halimah Abdullah, "Rights Hero Presses Plan for School in Detroit," *New York Times*, June 30, 1997.

21. The Michigan Coalition for Human Rights, http://www.mchr.org/mchr_history.html (accessed August 28, 2009).

22. Elaine Eason Steele, "A Personal Perspective: The Rosa and Raymond Parks Institute," http://brownvboard.org/brwnqurt/05–1/05–1b.htm (accessed August 28, 2009).

23. Brinkley, *Rosa Parks*, 215.

24. Rosa and Raymond Parks Institute for Self-Development, Program Overview, http://www.rosaparks.org/index.php?option=com_content&view=article&id=5&Itemid=5 (accessed August 29, 2009).

25. Bob Herbert, "In America; Mrs. Parks' Bequest," *New York Times*, September 4, 1994.

26. "Rights Leader Rosa Parks Attacked—Robber Injures 81-Year-Old At Her Home, Flees With $53," *Seattle Times*, http://community.seattletimes.nwsource.com/archive/?date=19940831&slug=1928057 (accessed August 29, 2009); "Man Arrested in Attack on Rights Pioneer Rosa Parks," *Los Angeles Times*, http://articles.latimes.com/1994–09–01/news/mn-33698_1_rights-pioneer-rosa-parks (accessed August 29, 2009).

27. Helen O'Neill, "Activist's Family Ponders Her Legacy," *Los Angeles Times*, December 12, 2004, A1.

28. Robert E. Tomasson, "Chronicle," *New York Times*, October 29, 1990; Susan Hiller Anderson, "Chronicle," *New York Times*, February 26, 1991; Nadine Brozan, "Chronicle," *New York Times*, November 7, 1994; Claire Shipman, "Rosa Parks Among 11 to Get Presidential Medal of Freedom," September 6, 1996, http://www.cnn.com/US/9609/06/pres.medal/index.html (accessed August 29, 2009); Gayle Pollard Terry,

"Rosa Parks; Still Fighting for Racial Justice—From the Front of the Bus," *Los Angeles Times*, April 19, 1998, 3.

29. Adam Clymer, "Rosa Parks Is Honored for Taking One Small Seat, One Giant Stand," *New York Times*, June 16, 1999; "Rosa Parks Honored With Congressional Gold Medal," CNN, http://www.cnn.com/US/9906/15/rosa.parks.medal/ (accessed August 29, 2009).

30. "Museum Honoring Rosa Parks Opens on Historic Street Corner," *New York Times*, December 2, 2000; "Rosa Parks's Home Put on Historic Register," *New York Times*, January 17, 2002.

31. "Rosa Parks Bus," The Henry Ford Museum, http://www.the henryford.org/exhibits/rosaparks/restoration.asp (accessed August 29, 2009).

32. Helen O'Neill, "Activist's Family Ponders Her Legacy," *Los Angeles Times*, December 12, 2004, A1.

33. Gary Sussman, "Bus Pass," http://www.ew.com/ew/article/0,,557904,00.html (accessed August 29, 2009); "Rosa Parks settles suit over OutKast CD," CNN, http://www.cnn.com/2005/SHOWBIZ/Music/04/15/parks.settlement/index.html (accessed August 29, 2009).

34. Helen O'Neill, "Activist's Family Ponders Her Legacy," *Los Angeles Times*, December 12, 2004, A1.

35. "Dennis Archer Appointed Guardian for Rosa Parks, Reviews Lawsuit," *Jet* (November 2004), http://findarticles.com/p/articles/mi_m1355/is_18_106/ai_n6358891/ (accessed April 1, 2011).

36. "Rosa Parks and Rap Duo OutKast Settle Lawsuit," *Jet*, http://findarticles.com/p/articles/mi_m1355/is_18_107/ai_n13819935/(accessed August 29, 2009).

37. E. R. Shipp, "Rosa Parks, 92, Founding Symbol of Civil Rights Movement, Dies," *New York Times*, October 25, 2005, http://www.nytimes.com/2005/10/25/national/25parks.html (accessed August 29, 2009).

CONCLUSION

Perhaps a headline in the *Montgomery Advertiser* best described Rosa Parks's funeral: "Pomp of Sendoff 'What She Deserved.'" On Saturday, October 29, hundreds of mourners stood along Norman Bridge Road and Patton Avenue in Montgomery to see the gray-and-white horse-drawn carriage that brought Rosa Parks's coffin to St. Paul AME Church. Fifteen white limousines followed the carriage. The passengers included Rosa Parks's longtime friend Johnnie Mae Carr and actress Cicely Tyson. Montgomery's State Representative Thad McClammy marched to the church as well. Young people lined the streets, many wiping tears from their eyes as the carriage passed them. Mourners from around the country—including California, Connecticut, and Tennessee—made the trip to Montgomery to honor Parks. "She left a legacy that all of us should be proud of. If it weren't for her, so many of us wouldn't be able to enjoy the rights we have today," said Andre Ellis.[1]

After the memorials in Montgomery, Parks's coffin was put aboard a Southwest Airlines flight and flown to Washington, D.C.—where Rosa Parks became one of only 30 Americans and the only private citizen and social activist in attendance—to lie in state in the Capitol Rotunda. Richard Baker, chief Senate historian said, "It's been a long road from that bus seat to the Capitol Rotunda in Washington. This is a great memorial to the courage of one person." After a memorial service at the Metropolitan AME Church, a Southwest Airlines plane piloted by one of the first African American commercial pilots flew Parks's coffin to Detroit.[2]

In Detroit, the first row of hundreds of city buses remained empty in memory of "all she had done on another bus miles from here 50 years ago." Politicians, civil rights leaders, famous musicians, ministers, and ordinary people, 4,000 in all, filled the Greater Grace Temple to honor Rosa Parks and hear the speeches. Many of those people had seen Parks over the years doing what she did best—speaking to their school class, attending a dedication, or at a community organization meeting. Thousands of people took the day off work waiting outside in the frigid early morning weather to see the antique, gold-trimmed horse-drawn carriage pass by, carrying Rosa Parks to Woodlawn Cemetery. A diverse array of dignitaries—including Reverend Jesse Jackson, Reverend Joseph Lowry, Reverend Al Sharpton, Louis Farrakhan, and former President Clinton—spoke to honor Parks and call others to action in her memory. "The woman we honored today held no public office, she wasn't a wealthy woman, didn't appear in the society pages," said Senator Barack Obama (D-Illinois). "And yet when the history of this country is written, it is this small, quiet woman whose name will be remembered long after the names of senators and presidents have been forgotten." The televised observance took more than six hours.[3]

The final years of Rosa Parks's life were filled with contention—not because of anything she did that was controversial; rather, controversy swirled around the role of her family and Elaine Eason Steele in her life. Parks's death did not alleviate the arguments; it only served to heighten the tensions. The battle over control of her estate had begun. Parks's will and trust named Elaine Eason Steele and Adam Shakoor, a retired judge, as administrators of her estate. William McCauley, Parks's nephew, filed a petition in Wayne County Probate Court demanding that the court name him as administrator instead. McCauley's lawyer said McCauley planned to protest the 2003 will because Parks was mentally incapacitated at the time she signed it. The family was upset with decisions Steele and Shakoor were making even before Parks's death. The McCauleys were troubled over the lawsuit filed on Parks's behalf and over the rap duo OutKast's use of her name in a song. They believed that Steele and Shakoor were using the suit for monetary gain.[4] The battle was not over the current assets of the estate but rather it was about future assets.

Who owned Rosa Parks's image? Who would profit from licensing her image? In 2006, licensing experts estimated that selling Parks's image, whether on t-shirts, coffee mugs, or posters, would bring in only six figures a year. Over time, however, licensing fees would bring in millions of dollars to whomever controlled her likeness. The Parks Institute, controlled by Steele and a beneficiary of the estate, hired CMG Worldwide, a company that specializes in celebrity licensing and merchandising, to market Parks's image. CMG negotiated an estimated six-figure deal with General Motors to use Parks's image in a Chevrolet commercial, along with other 1950s images.[5] The family and the executors of the estate were fighting over just this point.

According to Parks's will, her family members had no input into these decisions and the Parks Institute, under Steele's control, received

Rosa Parks, photographed in late November 1992 next to her own image in a mural commemorating the civil rights movement at the Dexter Avenue King Memorial Baptist Church in Montgomery. (AP Photo)

nearly all of the money. William McCauley said he became upset when, shortly after Parks's death, her image began to pop up in inappropriate places. One advertisement in the *Detroit Free Press* showed Parks along with the dates of her birth and death next to a logo for a local gambling business. "What a ride," the ad proclaimed. McCauley thought that was inappropriate. During her life, Rosa Parks decided when and where her image would be used. After her death, Steele agreed to relinquish control to McCauley in order to avoid a legal challenge from the family. That strategy was unsuccessful. The estate and the family could not come to an agreement about how to divide Parks's property, leading to a court battle. A judge removed Shakoor and McCauley as executors, replacing them with John Chase and Melvin Jefferson, two local lawyers.[6] In February 2007 the dispute ended when the parties reached an out-of-court settlement. In 2008, a Michigan probate court ordered that all Parks's assets be auctioned off and that the proceeds, which could total $10 million, be split between the Parks Institute and the family members. The AME Church and Alabama organizations expressed interest in the collection.[7]

Many things have been named for Rosa Parks since her death. In Montgomery, there is Rosa L. Parks Avenue, the Rosa Parks Branch of the Montgomery Library, the Rosa L. Parks Park, the Rosa Parks Quick Stop convenience store, Rosa Parks Place apartments, and the Rosa L. Parks Avenue Church of God. There is a short street named Rosa Parks Place, and there is the Troy University Rosa Parks Library and Museum. Everything from day care centers to schools carries Parks's name, from Miami, Florida, to Berkeley, California, and places in between. Even the Leigh Family Stable in Great Britain named a racehorse for Parks. In truth, many people do not even know why Rosa Parks's name was chosen for their buildings, streets, or parks. Cleveland Evans, an expert in onomastics—the study of names—believes it is hero worship. Evans is right.

Rosa Parks became a hero on December 1, 1955. Throughout her life and in death, Americans celebrated her for that one moment in time, as well they should have. Rosa Parks's refusal to give up her seat on that bus ignited a 381-day boycott, the longest civil rights action in American history. However, Parks's legacy includes more than that one moment. In her own way, Rosa Parks challenged Americas segregation system, both legal and customary, all of her life. She consistently resisted racism and fought for dignity and respect. Rosa Parks was a lifelong social and political activist who expanded American democracy and helped create a more just society.

NOTES

1. Erica Pippins and Jannell McGrew, "Pomp of Sendoff 'What She Deserved,'" *Montgomery Advertiser*, http://www.montgomeryadvertiser.com/apps/pbcs.dll/article?AID=/99999999/NEWS/61113009/1001 (accessed August 30, 2009).

2. Petula Dvorak and Hamil R. Harris, "Washington Prepares To Pay Rosa Parks Rare Tribute at Capitol," *Washington Post*, October 29, 2005.

3. Monica Davey, "In Detroit, a Day to Honor Rosa Parks," *New York Times*, November 3, 2005; "Rosa Parks Honored by Thousands at Funeral," http://www.msnbc.msn.com/id/9893832/ (accessed August 30, 2009).

4. Jeffrey Zaslow, "Rosa Parks's Death Stirs Up Bitter Feud Over Her Estate," *Wall Street Journal*, http://online.wsj.com/article_email/SB113210977500898576-lMyQjAxMDE1MzEyNjExMDY5Wj.html (accessed August 30, 2009); "Rosa Parks' Estate Triggers Battle," http://lawprofessors.typepad.com/trusts_estates_prof/2005/11/rosa_parks_esta.html (accessed August 30, 2009).

5. Jeremy W. Peters and Julie Bosman, "Rosa Parks Won a Fight, but Left a Licensing Rift," *New York Times*, October 8, 2006.

6. Ibid.

7. Paul Egan and Darren A. Nichols, "Rosa Parks' Estate Won't Be Fought For During a Trial," *Detroit News*, February 17, 2007; Adelle M. Banks, "Treasures, Tidbits All Up for Sale," *Washington Post*, July 26, 2008, B09.

SELECTED BIBLIOGRAPHY

BOOKS

Anderson, James. *Education of Blacks in the South 1860–1935*. Chapel Hill: University of North Carolina Press, 1988.

Branch, Taylor. *At Canaan's Edge: America in the King Years 1965–68*. New York: Simon and Schuster, 2006.

Branch, Taylor. *Parting the Waters: America in the King Years 1954–63*. New York: Simon and Schuster, 1989.

Brinkley, Douglas. *Rosa Parks; A Life*. New York: Penguin Books, 2000.

Brown, Sarah Hart. *Standing Against Dragons: Three Southern Lawyers in an Era of Fear*. Baton Rouge: Louisiana State University Press, 1998.

Burks, Mary Fair. "Trailblazers: Women in the Montgomery Bus Boycott." In *Black Women in United States History*, edited by Darlene Clark Hine. New York: Carlson Publishing, 1990.

Carson, Clayborne, ed. *The Papers of Martin Luther King, Jr.*: vol. IV. *Symbol of the Movement, January 1957–December 1958*. Berkeley: University of California Press, 2007.

Carter, Dan T. *Scottsboro: A Tragedy of the American South*. New York: Oxford University Press, 1969.

Chafe, William H. *Civilities and Civil Rights: Greensboro, North Carolina, and the Black Struggle for Freedom*. New York: Oxford University Press, 1981.

Chalmers, David H. *Hooded Americanism: The History of the Ku Klux Klan*, 3rd ed. Chapel Hill, NC: Duke University Press, 1987.

Clark, Septima. *Echo in My Soul*. New York: E. P. Dutton and Co., 1962.

Clark, Septima, and Cynthia Stokes Brown. *Ready from Within: A First Person Narrative*. Africa World Press; AWP edition, 1990.

Durr, Virginia Foster. *Outside the Magic Circle: The Autobiography of Virginia Foster Durr*. Reprint, Tuscaloosa: University of Alabama Press, 1990.

Franklin, John Hope, and Alfred A. Moss. *From Slavery to Freedom*, 8th ed. New York: McGraw Hill, 2000.

Garrow, David. *Bearing the Cross*. New York: Harper Perennial Modern Classics, 2004.

Gilbert, Olive. *Narrative of Sojourner Truth: A Bondswoman of Olden Time, With a History of Her Labors and Correspondence Drawn from Her Book of Life*. New York: Penguin Books, 1998.

Greenlee, Marcia M. "Interview with Rosa McCauley Parks" on August 22 and 23, 1978. In *The Black Woman Oral History Project*, vol. 8, edited by Ruth Edmonds Hill. Westport, CT: Meckler, 1991, 248.

Hanson, Joyce A. *Mary McLeod Bethune and Black Women's Political Activism*. Columbia: University of Missouri Press, 2003.

Harlan, Louis R. *Booker T. Washington*: vol. 1, *The Making of a Black Leader, 1856–1901*. New York: Oxford University Press, 1975.

Harlan, Louis R. *Booker T. Washington*: vol. 2, *The Wizard Of Tuskegee, 1901–1915*. New York: Oxford University Press, 1983.

Hart, Hastings H. "Social Problems of Alabama: A Study of the Social Institutions and Agencies of the State of Alabama Made at the Request of Governor Charles Henderson." New York: Russell Sage Foundation, 1918.

Higginbotham, Evelyn Brooks. *Righteous Discontent: The Women's Movement in the Black Baptist Church, 1880–1920*. Cambridge, MA: Harvard University Press, 1993.

Hine, Darlene Clark, ed. *Black Women in America*, 2nd ed., vol. 2. New York: Oxford University Press, 2005.

Hoose, Phillip. *Claudette Colvin: Twice Toward Justice*. Los Angeles: Farrar, Straus and Giroux, 2000.

Horowitz, David A. *Inside the Klavern: The Secret History of a Ku Klux Klan of the 1920s*. Carbondale, IL: Southern Illinois University Press, 1999.

Horton, Aimee Isgrig. *The Highlander Folk School: A History of Its Major Programs, 1932–1961*. New York: Carlson Publishing, 1989.

Horton, Myles. *The Long Haul: An Autobiography*. New York: Teachers College Press, 1998.

Jacobs, Dale. *The Myles Horton Reader: Education for Social Change*. Knoxville: University of Tennessee Press, 2003.

Jones, Thomas Jesse. "Negro Education: A Study of the Private and Higher Schools for Colored People in the United States," Phelps-Stokes Fund, vol. 2. Washington, DC: Government Printing Office, 1917.

Katz, Michael B. *"The Underclass Debate": Views from History*. Princeton, NJ: Princeton University Press, 1992.

King, Jr., Martin Luther. *Why We Can't Wait*. New York: Mentor, 1964.

Krueger, Thomas A. *And Promises to Keep: The Southern Conference for Human Welfare, 1938–1948*. Nashville, TN: Vanderbilt University Press, 1967.

MacLean, Nancy K. *Behind the Mask of Chivalry: The Making of the Second Ku Klux Klan*. New York: Oxford University Press, 1995.

McCullough, David. *Truman*. New York: Simon and Schuster, 1992.

McMurray, Linda O. *To Keep the Waters Troubled: The Life of Ida B. Wells*. New York: Oxford University Press, 1998.

McWhorter, Diane. *Carry Me Home: Birmingham, Alabama, The Climactic Battle of the Civil Rights Revolution*. New York: Simon and Schuster, 2001.

Marable, Manning, and Leith Mullings, ed. *Let Nobody Turn Us Around*. New York: Rowman and Littlefield, 2009.

Miller, James A. *Remembering Scottsboro: The Legacy of an Infamous Trial*. Princeton, NJ: Princeton University Press, 2009.

Oates, Stephen B. *Let the Trumpet Sound: A Life of Martin Luther King, Jr*. New York: Harper Perennial, 1994.

Olson, Lynne. *Freedom's Daughters: The Unsung Heroines of the Civil Rights Movement from 1830 to 1970*. New York: Simon and Schuster, 2001.

Ovington, Mary White. *The Walls Came Tumbling Down*. New York: Harcourt, Brace and Company; 1st stated edition, 1947.

Ovington, Mary White, and Ralph E. Luker. *Black and White Sat Down Together: The Reminiscences of an NAACP Founder*. New York: The Feminist Press at CUNY, 1996.

Parks, Rosa, with Jim Haskins. *My Story*. New York: Penguin Books, 1992.

Payne, Charles. "Men Led, but Women Organized: Movement Participation of Women in the Mississippi Delta," in *Women in the Civil Rights Movement: Trailblazers and Torchbearers, 1941–1964*, edited by Vicki L. Crawford, Jacqueline Anne Rouse, and Barbara Woods. New York: Carlson Publishing, 1990.

Pearson, Hugh. *When Harlem Nearly Killed King: The 1958 Stabbing of Dr. Martin Luther King, Jr.* New York: Seven Stories Press, 2004.

Ragsdale, Bruce A., and Joel D. Treese. *Black Americans in Congress, 1870–1989*. Washington: Diane Publishing, 2000.

Reed, Linda. *Simple Decency and Common Sense: The Southern Conference Movement, 1938–1963*. Bloomington: University of Indiana Press, 1991.

Robinson, JoAnn. *The Montgomery Bus Boycott and the Women Who Started It*. Knoxville: University of Tennessee Press, 1987.

Rosenberg, Gerald N. *The Hollow Hope: Can Courts Bring About Social Change?* 2nd ed. Chicago: University of Chicago Press, 2008.

Shapiro, Herbert. *White Violence and Black Response*. Cambridge, MA: University of Massachusetts Press, 1988.

Spivey, Donald. *Schooling for the New Slavery: Black Industrial Education, 1868–1915*. Westport, CT: Greenwood Press, 1978.

Sugrue, Thomas J. *The Origins of the Urban Crisis: Race and Inequality in Postwar Detroit*. Princeton, NJ: Princeton University Press, 2005.

Sullivan, Patricia, ed. *Freedom Writer: Virginia Foster Durr, Letters from the Civil Rights Years*. New York: Routledge, 2003.

Wadelington, Charles W., and Richard F. Knapp. *Charlotte Hawkins Brown and Palmer Memorial Institute: What One Young African American Woman Could Do*. Chapel Hill: University of North Carolina Press, 1999.

Washington, Booker T. "Industrial Education for the Negro." In *The Negro Problem*. New York: James Potts and Company, 1903.

White, Walter. *A Man Called White: The Autobiography of Walter White*. New York: Viking Press, 1948.

Whitfield, Stephen J. *A Death in the Delta: The Story of Emmett Till*. Baltimore: Johns Hopkins University Press, 1991.

Wiggington, Eliot. *Refuse to Stand Silently by: An Oral History of Grass Roots Social Activism in America, 1921–64*. New York: Doubleday, 1992.

Woodson, Carter G. *The Mis-education of the Negro*. Washington, DC: Associated Publishers, 1969.

MANUSCRIPT COLLECTIONS

E. D. Nixon Collection, Special Collections, Levi Watkins Library, Alabama State University, Montgomery.

Eugene W. Carter Papers, Alabama State Archives.

Montgomery Improvement Association Papers. Levi Watkins Learning Center, Alabama State University.

Rosa L. Parks Papers, Walter Reuther Archives of Labor and Urban Affairs, Wayne State University.

ARTICLES

Bush, Randall K. "Remembering Rosa Parks: Recognizing a Contemporary Prophetic Act." *Theological Studies*, vol. 65 (2004).

Elliott, Aprele. "Ella Baker: Free Agent in the Civil Right Movement." *Journal of Black Studies*, vol. 26, no. 5 (May 1996).

Enck, Henry S. "Black Self-Help in the Progressive Era: The 'Northern Campaigns' of Smaller Southern Black Industrial Schools, 1900–1915." *Journal of Negro History* 61, 1 (January 1976).

Gray, Eliza. "A Forgotten Contribution." *Newsweek* (March 2, 2009).

Greier, Peter. "Rosa Parks" Angry, Not Tired." *Dissent* (Winter 2006).

Gyant, LaVerne. "Passing the Torch: African American Women in the Civil Rights Movement." *Journal of Black Studies*, vol. 26, no. 5, Special Issue: The Voices of African American Women in the Civil Rights Movement (May 1996).

Hughes, Alvin C. "New Agenda for the South: The Role and Influence of the Highlander Folk School, 1953–1961." *Phylon*, vol. 46, no. 3 (1985).

Jansen, Donald. "Muslims Press Race Separation." *New York Times* (February 26, 1963).

Rowan, Carl T. "The Negro in the North." *Saturday Evening Post* (October 19, 1957): vol. 230, no. 16.

Washington, Booker T. "Chapters from My Experience." *World's Work* 21 (November 1910).

"X Marks the Spot." *Newsweek* (May 6, 1963).

NEWSPAPERS

Anderson, Susan Hiller. "Chronicle," *New York Times* (February 26, 1991).

Banks, Adelle M. "Treasures, Tidbits All Up for Sale," *Washington Post* (July 26, 2008), B09.

Brozan, Nadine. "Chronicle," *New York Times* (November 7, 1994).

Clymer, Adam. "Rosa Parks Is Honored for Taking One Small Seat, One Giant Stand," *New York Times* (June 16, 1999).

Davey, Monica. "In Detroit, a Day to Honor Rosa Parks," *New York Times* (November 3, 2005).

"Detroit Is Swept by Rioting and Fires; Romney Calls in Guard; 700 Arrested," *New York Times* (July 24, 1967).

Dvorak, Petula, and Hamil R. Harris. "Washington Prepares to Pay Rosa Parks Rare Tribute at Capitol," *Washington Post* (October 29, 2005).

Eblen, Tom. "Civil Rights Institution Fights for 'Economic Democracy'," *Los Angeles Times* (November 26, 1982).

Egan, Paul, and Darren A. Nichols. "Rosa Parks' Estate Won't Be Fought for During a Trial," *Detroit News* (February 17, 2007).

Herbert, Bob. "In America; Mrs. Parks' Bequest," *New York Times* (September 4, 1994).

Johnson, Thomas A. "'55 Montgomery Bus Boycott Marked," *New York Times* (December 8, 1975).

Loeb, Paul Rogat. "Commentary: Ordinary People Produce Extraordinary Results; Heroism: Rather Than Mythologize Those Who

Act for Justice, We Can Learn from What Empowered Them." *Los Angeles Times* (January 14, 2000).

"Malcolm X Woos 2 Rights Leaders," *New York Times* (May 19, 1964).

Martinez, Al. "'Mother of Civil Rights' a Reluctant Celebrity," *Los Angeles Times* (September 13, 1980), A1.

Mitchell, John. "Bus Ride That Moves a Nation Is Recalled," *Los Angeles Times* (January 25, 1991), Metro Section, 1.

"Museum Honoring Rosa Parks Opens on Historic Street Corner," *New York Times* (December 2, 2000).

O'Neill, Helen. "Activist's Family Ponders Her Legacy," *Los Angeles Times* (December 12, 2004), A1.

Peters, Jeremy W., and Julie Bosman. "Rosa Parks Won a Fight, but Left a Licensing Rift," *New York Times* (October 8, 2006).

Phillips, Wayne. "Negroes Pledge to Keep Boycott," *New York Times* (February 24, 1956).

Pippins, Erica, and Jannell McGrew. "Pomp Sendoff 'what she deserved'" *Montgomery Advertiser* (April 6, 2009).

"Rosa Parks's Home Put on Historic Register," *New York Times* (January 17, 2002).

Rubin, Richard. "The Ghosts of Emmett Till," *New York Times Magazine* (July 31, 2005).

Terry, Gayle Pollard. "Rosa Parks; Still Fighting for Racial Justice— From the Front of the Bus," *Los Angeles Times* (April 19, 1998).

Tomasson, Robert E. "Chronicle," *New York Times* (October 29, 1990).

"White Clergymen Urge Local Negroes to Withdraw from Demonstrations," *Birmingham News* (April 13, 1963).

WEBSITES

"African-American Soldiers in World War II Helped Pave Way for Integration of US Military," http://www.voanews.com/english/archive/2005–05/2005–05–10–voa47.cfm (Accessed July 15, 2009).

"Ancestors of Rosa (McCauley) Parks," ProGenealogists, http://www.progenealogists.com/parks/aqwg01.htm#1 (Accessed June 25, 2009).

"The Baton Rouge Bus Boycott of 1953...A Recaptured Past," http://www.lib.lsu.edu/special/exhibits/boycott/ (Accessed August 3, 2009).

Baulch, Vivian M., and Patricia Zacharias, "The 1943 Detroit Race Riots," *Detroit News*, http://apps.detnews.com/apps/history/index.php?id=185 (Accessed August 3, 2009).

The Birmingham Desegregation Campaign, http://www.amistadresource.org/civil_rights_era/birmingham_desegregation_campaign.html (Accessed August 23, 2009).

"The Chicago Defender," http://www.pbs.org/blackpress/news_bios/defender.html (Accessed August 20, 2009).

Children's Crusade, http://mlk-kpp01.stanford.edu/index.php/encyclopedia/encyclopedia/enc_childrens_crusade/ (Accessed August 23, 2009).

The Civil Rights Act of 1964 and the Equal Employment Opportunity Commission, http://www.archives.gov/education/lessons/civil-rights-act/ (Accessed August 24, 2009).

Constitution of Alabama, http://www.legislature.state.al.us/CodeOfAlabama/Constitution/1901/Constitution1901_toc.htm (Accessed July 16, 2009).

Davis, Angela. "Joan Little: The Dialectics of Rape" *Ms. Magazine*, http://www.msmagazine.com/spring2002/davis.asp (Accessed August 28, 2009).

E. D. Nixon, http://www.encyclopediaofalabama.org/face/Article.jsp?id=h-1355 (Accessed July 17, 2009).

Elaine Eason Steele Biography, http://www.rosaparks.org/index.php?option=com_content&view=article&id=24&Itemid=34 (Accessed August 21, 2009).

"End of U.S. Military Segregation Set Stage for Rights Movement," http://www.america.gov/st/peopleplace-english/2008/February/20080225120859liameruoy0.9820215.html (Accessed August 1, 2009).

Famous American Trials, http://www.law.umkc.edu/faculty/projects/Ftrials/scottsboro/scottsb.htm (Accessed July 9, 2009).

Garfield, Bob, An Interview with Timothy Tyson, "Tabula Rosa," http://www.onthemedia.org/transcripts/2009/07/03/02 (Accessed August 25, 2009).

Gibson, Robert A., "The Negro Holocaust: Lynching and Race Riots in the United States,1880–1950," Yale-New Haven Teachers Institute, http://www.yale.edu/ynhti/curriculum/units/1979/2/79.02.04.x.html, (Accessed June 25, 2009).

Goodman, Amy, "John Conyers On Rosa Parks: "She Earned the Title as Mother of the Civil Rights Movement." http://www.democracynow.org/2005/10/25/john_conyers_on_rosa_parks_she (Accessed August 24, 2009).

"A Half-Century of Learning: Historical Statistics on Educational Attainment in the United States, 1940 to 2000" http://www.census.gov/population/www/socdemo/education/phct41.html (Accessed July 13, 2009).

Harry S. Truman Library and Museum, http://www.trumanlibrary.org/whistlestop/study_collections/desegregation/large/index.php (Accessed August 1, 2009).

Highlander Research and Education Center, http://www.highlandercenter.org/a-history.asp (Accessed August 12, 2009).

"History of the NAACP," http://www.naacp.org/about/history/timeline/index.htm (Accessed July 27, 2009).

"HU Mourns the Loss of Rosa Parks," http://www.hamptonu.edu/news/102605_27_rosa_parks.htm (Accessed August 21, 2009).

The King Center, "Commemorative Service," http://www.thekingcenter.org/KingHoliday/Commemorative.aspx (Accessed August 28, 2009).

Krause, Lisa, "Black Soldiers in WW II: Fighting Enemies at Home and Abroad." National Geographic News (February 15, 2001), http://news.nationalgeographic.com/news/2001/02/0215_tuskegee.html (Accessed July 15, 2009).

Ku Klux Klan Act, http://law.jrank.org/pages/8020/Ku-Klux-Klan-Act.html (Accessed June 29, 2009).

Linder, Douglas O. The Trial of "The Scottsboro Boys," Famous American Trials, http://www.law.umkc.edu/faculty/projects/Ftrials/scottsboro/scottsb.htm (Accessed July 9, 2009).

Lohr, Kathy, "FBI Re-Examines 1946 Lynching Case," http://www.npr.org/templates/story/story.php?storyId=5579862 (Accessed August 1, 2009).

Louisiana State Museum, http://lsm.crt.state.la.us/post-ed8.htm (Accessed August 4, 2009).

Major Features of the Civil Rights Act of 1964, http://www.congress link.org/print_basics_histmats_civilrights64text.htm (Accessed August 27, 2009).

"Man Arrested in Attack on Rights Pioneer Rosa Parks," *Los Angeles Times*, http://articles.latimes.com/1994–09–01/news/mn-33698_1_rights-pioneer-rosa-parks (Accessed August 29, 2009).

"The March on Washington," http://www.core-online.org/History/washington_march.htm (Accessed August 24, 2009).

Martin Luther King, Jr., Papers. http://www.stanford.edu/group/King/papers/ (Accessed August 18, 2009).

McGrew, Jannell, "Aurelia Shines Browder Coleman," *Montgomery Advertiser*, http://www.montgomeryboycott.com/profile_browder.htm (Accessed August 17, 2009).

Mayhem in the City: The Detroit Riots, http://www.npr.org/tem plates/story/story.php?storyId=12195165 (Accessed August 26, 2009).

The Michigan Coalition for Human Rights, http://www.mchr.org/mchr_history.html (Accessed August 28, 2009).

The Montgomery Bus Boycott, http://www.watson.org/~lisa/black history/civilrights-55–65/montbus.html (Accessed August 19, 2009).

NAACP v. Alabama, http://www.oyez.org/cases/1950–1959/1957/1957_91 (Accessed August 11, 2009).

National Association for the Advancement of Colored People in Alabama, http://www.encyclopediaofalabama.org/face/Article.jsp?id=h-1670 (Accessed July 15, 2009).

National Association of Colored Women, http://www.nacwc.org/about/objectives.php (Accessed August 24, 2009).

National Council of Negro Women, http://www.ncnw.org/index.htm (accessed August 24, 2009).

"1963 March on Washington: 'Freedom' The Demands, The Pledge, The Prayer," http://forum-network.org/node/1267 (Accessed August 24, 2009).

Nonviolent Resistance, http://mlk-kpp01.stanford.edu/index.php/en cyclopedia/encyclopedia/enc_nonviolent_resistance/ (Accessed August 25, 2009).

North Carolina History Project, "Greensboro Sit-In," http://www. northcarolinahistory.org/encyclopedia/299/entry (Accessed August 23, 2009).

Pippins, Erica, and Jannell McGrew, "Pomp of Sendoff 'What She Deserved'," *Montgomery Advertiser*, http://www.montgomery advertiser.com/apps/pbcs.dll/article?AID=/99999999/NEWS/ 61113009/1001 (Accessed August 30, 2009).

President Lyndon B. Johnson's Address to the Nation, March 31, 1968, http://www.lbjlib.utexas.edu/Johnson/archives.hom/speeches. hom/680331.asp (Accessed August 26, 2009).

Price, Mary, "Baton Rouge Bus Boycott Background," http://www.lib. lsu.edu/special/exhibits/boycott/background.html (Accessed August 4, 2009).

Report of the National Advisory Commission on Civil Disorders, http:// www.eisenhowerfoundation.org/docs/kerner.pdf (Accessed August 26, 2009).

"Rights Leader Rosa Parks Attacked—Robber Injures 81-Year-Old At Her Home, Flees With $53," *Seattle Times*, http://community. seattletimes.nwsource.com/archive/?date=19940831&slug=192 8057 (Accessed August 29, 2009).

The Rise and Fall of Jim Crow, http://www.pbs.org/wnet/jimcrow/stories_ events_tuskegee.html (Accessed June 25, 2009).

Robert F. Kennedy Assassination (Summary), http://foia.fbi.gov/foiain dex/rfkasumm.htm (Accessed August 27, 2009).

Rosa and Raymond Parks Institute for Self-Development, Program Overview, http://www.rosaparks.org/index.php?option=com_ content&view=article&id=5&Itemid=5 (Accessed August 29, 2009).

"Rosa McCauley," *Africana Studies*, Department of Africana Studies at Stony Brook University, Stony Brook, NY, http://www.sunysb. edu/afs/?afsphotos/rparks (Accessed August 28, 2009).

"Rosa Parks Bus," The Henry Ford Museum, http://www.thehenry ford.org/exhibits/rosaparks/restoration.asp (Accessed August 29, 2009).

"Rosa Parks' Estate Triggers Battle," http://lawprofessors.typepad.com/ trusts_estates_prof/2005/11/rosa_parks_esta.html (Accessed August 30, 2009).

"Rosa Parks honored by thousands at funeral," http://www.msnbc.msn.com/id/9893832/ (Accessed August 30, 2009).

"Rosa Parks honored with Congressional Gold Medal," CNN, http://www.cnn.com/US/9906/15/rosa.parks.medal/ (Accessed August 29, 2009).

Rosa Parks interview, Sound Roll 1525, Camera Roll 557, http://www.teachersdomain.org/resource/iml04.soc.ush.civil.parks/Transcript, 3 (Accessed August 18, 2009).

"Rosa Parks settles suit over OutKast CD," CNN, http://www.cnn.com/2005/SHOWBIZ/Music/04/15/parks.settlement/index.html (Accessed August 29, 2009).

Sarah Mae Flemming, Appellant, v. South Carolina Electric and Gas Company, a Corporation, Appellee, United States Court of Appeals Fourth Circuit.—224 F.2d 752, http://cases.justia.com/us-court-of-appeals/F2/224/752/145976/ (Accessed August 14, 2009.

Shipman, Claire, "Rosa Parks among 11 to get Presidential Medal of Freedom," September 6, 1996, http://www.cnn.com/US/9609/06/pres.medal/index.html, (Accessed August 29, 2009).

Shipp, E. R., "Rosa Parks, 92, Founding Symbol of Civil Rights Movement, Dies," *New York Times*, (October 25, 2005), http://www.nytimes.com/2005/10/25/national/25parks.html (Accessed August 29, 2009).

Simkins, Chris, Martin Luther King, Jr., Remembered on 40th Anniversary of Assassination, http://www.voanews.com/english/archive/2008–04/2008–04–03-voa29.cfm?moddate=2008–04–03 (Accessed August 26, 2009).

South Carolina African American History Online, http://www.scafricanamerican.com/honorees/view/2008/5/ (Accessed August 14, 2009).

"Southern Christian Leadership Conference," *The New Georgia Encyclopedia*, http://www.georgiaencyclopedia.org/nge/Article.jsp?id=h-2743 (Accessed August 23, 2009).

"The Southern Manifesto," From *Congressional Record*, 84th Congress Second Session, vol. 102, part 4 (March 12, 1956). Washington, DC: Government Printing Office, 1956: 4459–60, http://www.strom.clemson.edu/strom/manifesto.html (Accessed August 4, 2009).

"Speech at the Great March on Detroit," http://mlk-kpp01.stanford. edu/index.php/kingpapers/article/speech_at_the_great_march_ on_detroit/ (Accessed August 24, 2009).

"The Spingard Medal," http://www.naacp.org/events/spingarn/index. htm (Accessed August 28, 2009).

"The Springfield Race Riot of 1908," www.visit-springfieldillinois. com/.../1908-RaceRiot-Brochure.pdf (Accessed July 27, 2009).

Sussman, Gary, "Bus Pass," http://www.ew.com/ew/article/0,,557904,00. html (Accessed August 29, 2009).

Teaching With Documents: An Act of Courage, The Arrest Records of Rosa Parks, The National Archives, http://www.archives.gov/ education/lessons/rosa-parks/ (Accessed August 17, 2009).

Transcript of Civil Rights Act (1964), http://www.ourdocuments. gov/doc.php?doc=97&page=transcript (Accessed August 24, 2009).

"Trials: Joan Little's Story," *Time* magazine, http://www.time.com/time/ magazine/article/0,9171,913413,00.html (Accessed August 28, 2009).

U.S. Supreme Court, *Brown v. Board of Education*, 347 U.S. 483 (1954), http://caselaw.lp.findlaw.com/scripts/getcase.pl?court= us&vol=347&invol=483 (Accessed August 4, 2009).

U.S. Supreme Court, *Henderson v. United States*, 339 U.S. 816 (1950) 339 U.S. 816 http://laws.findlaw.com/us/339/816.html (Accessed August 10, 2009).

U.S. Supreme Court, *NAACP v. Alabama*, 377 U.S. 288 (1964) http:// laws.findlaw.com/us/377/288.html (Accessed August 11, 2009).

Voting Rights Act of 1965, http://www.congresslink.org/print_basics_ histmats_votingrights_contents.htm (Accessed August 27, 2009).

Walker, Tim, "*Browder v. Gayle*: The Women Before Rosa Parks," http://www.tolerance.org/teach/activities/activity.jsp?cid=388 (Accessed August 17, 2009).

White, Walter (1893–1955), http://www.georgiaencyclopedia.org/nge/ Article.jsp?id=h-747 (Accessed July 16, 2009).

Zaslow, Jeffrey. "Rosa Parks's Death Stirs Up Bitter Feud Over Her Estate," *Wall Street Journal*, http://online.wsj.com/article_email/ SB113210977500898576-lMyQjAxMDE1MzEyNjExMDY5Wj. html (Accessed August 30, 2009).

DOCUMENTARY

PBS, American Experience—"Scottsboro: An American Tragedy," directed by Barak Goodman and Daniel Anker, 90 minutes (2000).

INDEX

About the Author

JOYCE A. HANSON is professor of history at California State University at San Bernardino. She is the author of *Mary McLeod Bethune and Black Women's Political Activism* (2003) and numerous articles in professional journals, chiefly on African American history and women's history.